The Snow Leopard's New Friend

Michael Buckley

Contents

Preface by Geshe Lhakdor	4
Introduction: Eco-Tales from Tibet	5

Stories

The Snow Leopard's New Friend	9
Red Panda Hiccups	17
The Griffon who Set off to See the World	23
The Antelope Detective	31
The Angry Bear	39
The Big-hearted Takin	47
Songs of the Wild Yak	57
Crazy Old Sand Fox	65
The Unexpected Otter	75
Dancing like a Crane: a true story from Bhutan	83

eXTreme Animals from Tibet — 89

profiles of animals featured in this book, in chapter order—from Snow Leopard to Black-necked Crane

Get Involved! — 111

following up with questions, discussion & resources
cross-language connections, copyright & credit notices

Preface

by Geshe Lhakdor

Tibetan people's belief in the sacredness of its natural environment—coupled with their profound wisdom and skill to co-exist harmoniously with its surrounding environment—has helped in the conservation of the world's highest plateau until the Chinese occupation in 1959. Successive rulers in Tibet issued strict prohibitions on hunting and felling of trees at important ecological sites. But with the Chinese occupation, Tibet witnessed sudden disruption in its age-old tradition of causing minimum harm to the natural environment and its wildlife inhabitants.

At this critical period, Michael Buckley's book *The Snow Leopard's New Friend*: Tibetan Animal Tales is timely. The stories of animals like the elusive Snow Leopard, prowling its inhospitable region in the Tibetan plateau, the Black-necked Crane, the last crane species to be discovered, and the Tibetan Antelope with its fine *shahtoosh* wool are all extraordinary Tibetan animals featured here.

We learn from our elders, the great respect they paid for wildlife and which has become a part of Tibetan culture. We are heavily dependent upon the environment in which we live and we cannot think of an environment devoid of these beautiful animals and birds.

I therefore thank Michael for giving this gift to the children about our Tibetan animal friends who are today facing threat of total extinction. If there is one factor that helps us all live in harmony and happiness that one factor is unconditional love, for everything that exists, based on a larger perspective of how everything on this planet is bound together by a network of mutual dependency. Friends, wake up before it is too late!

> —Geshe Lhakdor is the Director of the Library of Tibetan Works & Archives, Dharamsala, India. He has arranged for this book to be translated into the Tibetan language for print publication in India and as a Tibetan digital edition.

Eco-Tales from Tibet

What can be cuter than a Snow Leopard cub? A small cat at first, but one that will grow into an extraordinary creature. Superbly adapted to snow and altitude, the Snow Leopard makes its home in one of the most inhospitable regions on earth—the Tibetan plateau.

The Snow Leopard is so elusive that it was not captured on movie film until the dawn of the 21st century. The Black-necked Crane was the last of the 15 crane species to be discovered, due to its remote habitat. The Tibetan Antelope has evolved with the finest wool on the planet—designed to protect it at freezing temperatures. The connection between the Tibetan Antelope and the fine wool *shahtoosh* was only revealed in the 1990s. The extraordinary Tibetan animals featured in this short book have each found novel ways to survive the extreme cold, the wind, the snow, the altitude.

Great respect for wildlife has long been part of Tibetan culture. The pre-Buddhist religion of Tibet was Bon, an animist faith with belief in spirits dwelling in mountains, trees, rivers and lakes—and in animals.

Shamans invoked animal spirits at ceremonies—traditions still found in Mongolia. Tibetan Buddhism is unique in that it imported Bon beliefs into Buddhism.

Over 2,400 years ago, in India, one of the earliest of the Buddhist scriptures to appear was the *Jataka Tales*. This collection of 547 poems depicts the previous lives or incarnations of the Buddha in both human and animal form. Written up in Sanskrit and Pali, these tales made the rounds of the Buddhist world—with translation into various languages, including Tibetan. His Holiness the Dalai Lama gives an annual teaching on selected *Jataka Tales*.

HH Dalai Lama reading from the *Jataka Tales*, March 2017 *Photo by Tenzin Choejor/OHHDL*

The *Jataka Tales* comprise a series of moral fables, setting up problems and dilemmas that are solved though ingenuity, compassion and logic. And through use of a moral compass.

The Snow Leopard's New Friend also targets compassionate solutions—about the environment. Since the 1950s, Tibet's environment has fallen on hard times under Chinese occupation. The grasslands have been ravaged by rampant mining. The rivers have been blocked by megadams.

The glaciers are melting quickly—most due to a rain of black soot from fossil fuels in both China and India. The arrival of the railway from Qinghai to Tibet, reaching Lhasa in 2006, has accelerated China's exploitation of Tibet, meaning the exploitation of its vast mineral resources, its powerful rivers, its abundant groundwater, its sacred lakes and pristine mountain landscapes.

And now, time to read on, about those cute Snow Leopard cubs—and their very worried mother…

Lama Mani, a roving Tibetan storyteller who can recite entire legends from memory, and who uses thangka and texts to narrate stories out loud. Now rare to see in the Tibetan world.

The Snow Leopard's New Friend

*All done and dusted,
it's a matter of being trusted...*

Ladakh, India, bordering Tibet

The Snow Leopard is very confused. Her foot has been caught in an agonising trap close to her lair, high in the snows. She must do something—or she will die here and so will her two cubs. And then, through the snow comes a mysterious human and darts her with something, and she collapses, drugged, but not entirely out. She can still make out blurry shapes. The human is trying to remove the trap from her foot. Now she is really confused—one human has laid a trap to kill her, and yet this other human is trying to rescue her.

The human, Dorjee, knows the answer to this dilemma, but has no way to communicate with the big cat. He is a wildlife researcher, studying the behaviour of snow leopards. But they are so elusive he has only caught fleeting glimpses of them. The ghost cat, as snow leopards are sometimes called, is very stealthy. And he is well aware that the leopards are doing all the observation: they are watching him, not the opposite. He knows the man who laid the trap. He is a Chinese gold miner, who seeks extra income from hunting the snow leopard, whose pelt will bring a pretty price.

Now he examines the snow leopard's foot. It is free, but it is damaged. A foot like that could take months to heal before she can get back up to hunting speed and out-run a blue sheep or an ibex over mountain terrain. She cannot hunt, which means her newborn cubs will starve to death.

Dorjee retreats to a well-hidden position and watches the snow leopard revive through powerful binoculars. He follows her all the way to her cave, and notes the exact position. Night falls. Dorjee has christened her 'Kaba', one of the Tibetan words for 'snow.'

The next morning, Dorjee is back at the cave with a gift—fresh meat from the butcher. He needs to win Kaba's trust. No easy ride. The leopard has nearly been killed by a human, so how can she possibly determine which humans are trustworthy?

Kaba cannot believe her eyes. How did this meat miraculously get here? She limps over, sniffs at it, and sets about dragging the meat back to her cubs in the cave.

A week later, just as the cubs are gnawing at the last bits of bone, more meat shows up near the cave. But this time, Kaba has been on the lookout. She has sharp eyes, even in dim light. And as Dorjee is about to drop the meat, he sees Kaba in the distance, in the darkness of her cave, almost invisible except for her pale blue eyes. For a few seconds, their eyes lock. But

it feels like an eternity to Dorjee. It feels like the leopard is scanning his very soul for the answer to her questions: Can I trust you? Is this another trap? But Kaba knows that without this meat home delivery she will perish—and so will her cubs. She has to take this chance.

The weeks pass. More gifts of meat. More time passing, more meat. And as time passes, a subtle change is under way. Dorjee no longer tries to conceal his presence when he comes to the cave. One day, to his shock and delight, two cubs rush out, bounding toward him and the meat. They have no fear, no hesitation like their mother. They just want to play. Dorjee takes photos of them. And then he looks around to see Kaba sitting on the snow, with her tail wrapped around her, watching him. She has finally accepted his presence, and she has given him a mother's seal of approval—by allowing her precious cubs to go forward to greet him.

The weeks pass, turning into months, turning into summer. Kaba is stronger again, testing out her foot, chasing her cubs around. The spring is back in her legs. She is ready to hunt again.

Kaba's cave is in the middle of nowhere, but unknown to her, it sits on the borderlands of Ladakh and Tibet. The cave is right inside a nature reserve. Dorjee wants this region to be expanded into a larger reserve where snow leopards can roam freely. But miners are moving in, on both sides of the border, looking for gold and precious metals. They are in no mood to let a few snow leopards get in their way—nor in the mood to have Dorjee set up a larger nature reserve that would keep them out.

Snow leopard pelts are worth a lot more on the Tibetan side, where Chinese miners hunt them for extra income. But first they have to find them. The snow leopard is so stealthy that it is practically invisible in snowy terrain.

Dorjee is out on his motorbike toward dusk, monitoring the area. In the distance is a miner taking aim at him with a hunting gun—intended for snow leopards. The miner is next to his jeep.

Snow leopards are excellent leapers. They have to be—in order to catch blue sheep. Kaba springs into action. She races toward the jeep and takes an enormous leap, crashing into the miner and knocking him to the ground just as the gun fires.

A loud gunshot echoes across the valley. Dorjee scans with his binoculars and is astonished to find Kaba with teeth bared, standing over the terrified miner. Dorjee turns his motorcycle and speeds over, grabs the hunter's gun and smashes it on the rocks.

He realises that Kaba has just saved his life, the same way he saved her life. She has returned the favour. And he knows he is very lucky.

Dorjee checks the map. The Chinese miner and his jeep are on the Ladakhi side of the border. So he ties up the miner, under arrest for poaching inside a nature reserve, and confiscates his jeep. Kaba and her cubs are safe as long as they remain on the Ladakh side of the border, but snow leopards have no idea of borders. They will roam their territory.

Realising that photos of Kaba and her cubs are the key to getting donations to expand the nature reserve and to employ more rangers to patrol, Dorjee works hard on unusual angles. His photos win top prizes in international competitions. He wins the Wildlife Photographer of the Year award.

The arrest of the Chinese miner creates an international incident, with lots of press coverage. China is infuriated, and demands the immediate return of the miner. India protests that the miner crossed into Indian territory. A press circus rages. Finally, the miner is returned to the Tibetan side, minus his jeep.

Snow leopards are solitary and secretive, rarely making friends among their own species. But this snow leopard has made a new friend. A friend that she completely trusts.

Along with that trust, Dorjee gets fantastic opportunities to shoot mother and cubs—with a camera. A selfie with them goes viral on Facebook and Instagram, getting hundreds of thousands of hits. As Dorjee explains the situation of this snow leopard and her cubs, and others like her, donations roll in to create a conservation area. Dorjee convinces local miners that there is more money to be made for their families in tourism, small lodges and hiking tours.

Ladakh has ice stupas—pyramid-shaped structures that mimic what a glacier does, with slow dripping of water. Inside one of these structures is the cave-like Ice Stupa Café, with a few chairs. Dorjee has enticed Kaba and her cubs to sit inside the Ice Stupa Café for a photo opportunity. Snow leopards like caves, after all. And ice. And snow. That's the photo that goes viral—with donations flooding in.

Insight

Will the Snow Leopard become as mythical as the Snow Lion?

Red Panda Hiccups

A shocking story about a small panda with a big problem

Yunnan, Southwest China

Tashi the Red Panda lay clutching his belly in the bamboo forest that grew near the farmer's hot red pepper patch.

Hic! hic! Hic!

"Tashi, have you been gorging on the red peppers again? How many times have I told you to stay away from those peppers!"

"It's okay Dad, this will *Hic! Hic!* stop soon."

But it didn't. The hiccupping went on well into the night, keeping everyone awake. And Tashi was having trouble eating, as the hiccupping had hurt his tummy. "Son, why did you eat those red peppers again? You know what happened last time!"

"I can't explain it, Dad. The peppers are so *hic hic hic!* delicious, and I just forgot about what they can do to me."

As the *hic! Hic! Hic!* went on into the third night, Tashi's mother and father were fighting exhaustion from lack of sleep. The neighbours were complaining, saying the loud hiccupping was keeping them awake too—to the point where they were missing out on their precious Dreamtime. Dreaming of luxurious leafy bamboo, and great forests to roam in.

Since he couldn't sleep because of the hiccups, Tashi could only day-dream. All about Lolha, a beautiful redhead who lived down the valley. Long ringed tail, bushy and full, and fluttering eyelids. Her smile melted Tashi's heart and made him feel weak in the knees. He dreamed of saying: "Lolha, I *hic! hic! Hic!* love you! I want to *hic! Hic! hic!* spend my days with you!" Daytime nightmare. She gave him the Death Stare, and climbed higher into the trees.

Tashi tried everything to cure the hiccups. Standing on his head and breathing quickly. Rapidly drinking water while squeezing his nose. Pulling on his tongue. Breathing out while pinching his nose. Taking a large gulp of air, holding it, and breathing slowly out. Squeezing his palms hard together.

But nothing worked…

In utter desperation, his parents decided to consult the Red Panda Master—the oldest and wisest among them. They found him in a tall tree, quietly taking in the sublime mountain views, but perhaps secretly having a nap. Tashi's parents explained the problem. The Master thought this over for some time, playing with his long spindly whiskers.

Finally, he advised them: "You must give Tashi a great shock. The bigger the shock, the better." And he added, cryptically: "Then you will see the light of day. But not without a few hiccups."

And so Tashi's parents set off on a mission to scare the living

daylights out of him. First stop: a journey to the edge of the forest. Where massive clearing of trees was under way. Not a single tree spared. All reduced to stumps. Tashi gasped.

"But we cannot *Hic! hic!* live without trees!"

"That's right," said his parents. "Without trees, no access to food. No shade, no protection. And no escape from predators."

"So why are they cutting down all the *hic! hic! Hic!* trees?"

"To make their homes and things to sit on, and things to store other things. And to make the eating things, the long thin sticks the humans eat with."

"But they are destroying our *hic! Hic!* homes to make their homes."

"Yes, son, destroying our world to make their world. And this way, destroying all life that depends on trees—for the shade and shelter and food they bring."

Tashi was deeply shocked by this—but not enough to cure his *hic! Hic! Hic!* hiccupping. His parents desperately tried to arrange more shocking situations.

Nothing seemed to work.

Finally, Tashi's Dad came up with a brilliant tactical plan—a rather gruesome one.

"Let's take him to see Uncle Jorten and Aunt Bhuti!" Tashi's Mum was horrified.

"He's too young for that!" She cried.

"We have exhausted all the options. And nobody is getting any sleep," said his father. "We have to do this."

They both approached Tashi.

"Do you remember Uncle Jorten and his wife Bhuti?"

"Of course! The ones who *Hic! hic!* disappeared five months ago? My favourite uncle and aunt. So *hic! Hic!* kind and generous."

"Well, we found them, at last."

"Really? Where?!"

That night it wasn't only the hiccups that kept Tashi awake. Tashi was beyond excited about seeing Uncle Jorten and Aunt

Bhuti again. The following morning, he eagerly followed his parents to the outskirts of a human town.

They found a perch in a tree overlooking a square in the town. To one side, humans were having their photos taken in ethnic dress, which consisted of colourful robes, old rifles, and some fur hats. Each hat was made from a skin, with a long ringed tail hanging down. Those could only be Red Panda skins. Tashi's jaw dropped. Tashi could only see the backs of the humans waiting to have their photos taken.

Then the humans turned to the camera, their hats revealing the heads of Uncle Jorten and Aunt Bhuti at the front of the skins. Lifeless heads, with glazed eyeballs. Made of glass beads.

Tashi wanted to scream. But he was so shocked to his core that no sound came out of his mouth. Not even a hiccup.

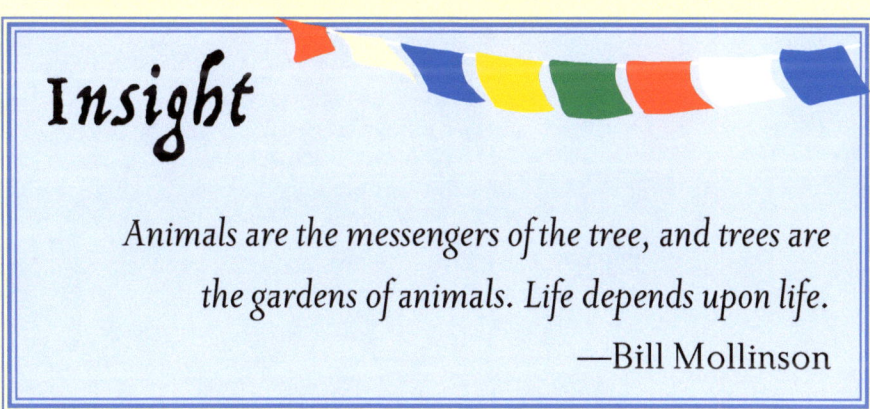

Insight

Animals are the messengers of the tree, and trees are the gardens of animals. Life depends upon life.
—Bill Mollinson

The Griffon Who Set Off To See The World

A high-flying tale about spreading your wings

Central Tibet

After her seventh failed attempt to cross the Himalayan peaks, Karlha decided to seek out some expert help.

Normally unflappable, this Himalayan Griffon was at the end of her patience. Wings icing up. Powerful headwinds. Lack of dead animals to dine on at higher altitudes.

Karlha got her nickname from being very curious—at an early age—about absolutely everything. Her head was in the stars all the time, always dreaming. She asked her parents a relentless string of questions. *Why is the sky blue? How high can griffons fly? Why do griffons only eat dead meat? Just how dangerous are eagles? How do griffons manage to stay up in the air for hours?*

But the question that stumped all the griffons was this one: *What lies across the snow-capped mountains?*

Nobody knew the answer to that because no griffon had ever flown across the mountains. They were all content to stay in Tibet.

"But we have enormous wings!" Karlha cried. "We can fly everywhere!"

In response, Karlha was repeatedly warned about the dangers of the unknown land to the south. Many dangers. Humans with shooting sticks. Poisoned dead animals.

Dangerous eagles. But her mind was set. She wanted to do everything, and she wanted to go everywhere. A wildly impulsive bird who just wanted to see the world. Have wings, will travel. Nothing else needed—just some dead animals to eat along the way. She perfected the art of gliding—staying up in the air by riding the hot air currents. She would get over those mountains, no matter what the other griffons warned her about.

Karlha spotted a flock of Bar-headed Geese headed for a high pass. Maybe they could help with her quest? But the geese honked and honked and rapidly flew off, afraid of Karlha's enormous wingspan. She looked like a Golden Eagle, a large predator that attacks other birds—even foxes.

Karlha made friends with a Snow Pigeon, who confirmed that the Bar-headed Geese indeed flew over the Himalayan peaks, not once but twice a year. Karlha was beyond excited. But she still could not get close to the geese. Finally the Snow Pigeon convinced the geese that griffons only eat dead meat—they are scavengers, not predators.

"How can we tell the difference?" asked a goose.

"The griffon is ugly and has a bald head," replied the

Snow Pigeon.

The geese all giggled at this, but they started to see the difference. Then another problem arose: the geese could not understand the griffon's thick western Tibetan accent. So the Snow Pigeon acted as her chirpy translator.

The Bar-headed Geese finally accepted Karlha's request to join them, but indicated they would not stop for her.

First big surprise: take-off at night, toward dawn. Take-off in a V pattern with strongest in the lead. But not straight over a mountain top as Karlha expected. They detoured a long way to a mountain pass. Where Golden Eagles lay in ambush. The formation was attacked by these large eagles, who knew the migration route well. The geese carried on, a few less in number.

With the freezing cold and icy headwinds, Karlha was not sure she would make it. She had to use every ounce of flying strength to keep up.

But finally they crossed the high peaks and descended into a deep green valley. So many shades of green! Way more than Tibet. And different animals to dine on.

Strange ones with no coats, not hairy like the animals in Tibet. Yaks without coats. She found out the names. Buffalo was one, and another one called Cow.

In Nepal, Karlha overdid it on the dead cow. Feasted on it, and got into big trouble. Little humans throwing rocks. On a full stomach, she could not take off—she was too heavy for lift-off. But she could not run fast enough to get away from little humans. Finally, big humans captured her. They kept her for five days with no food, then took her to a mountain top. She ran down the slope and soared into the air, free at last.

But she was soon buzzed by a cranky Serpent Eagle, who zoomed past at lightning speed. A big bird with spotty feathers and yellow beak.

"Buzz off!" Shouted the eagle. "This is my territory!"

"This is open air," protested Karlha, angrily. "It should be free for all birds to fly through."

"You see that nest down there?" Sneered the Serpent Eagle. "All the air above that nest is mine! Now move along before I rip you apart, you silly buzzard!"

It was strange for a bird to own a territory of air, but

the Serpent Eagle looked fierce, and Karlha quickly winged along, heading south—to India.

She got terribly sick in India. At first from air pollution, but later from the meat. Zonked out. Dizzy. Blurred vision.

The world spinning. When she finally snapped out of this state, her eyes focused on the finest Griffon she had ever seen. Magnificent talons, steady gaze in the eyes.

"Are you okay?"

"Not the best," she replied, weakly. The buzzard detected a funny accent.

"You're new, aren't you? Where are you from?"

"Tibet."

"Whoah! A rare bird indeed!"

He scanned her features, confirming she was indeed an exotic creature.

"So that explains something. You don't have dead cows up there, right?"

"Correct. We have dead yaks, goats, wild critters."

"Better be careful what animals you eat here. Allow me to show you around. My name is Vikram. What's yours?"

They took to the air.

"You see, crazy farmers feed drugs to their cows when they get sick, and if you eat one of those cows, that could be your last meal. All around this region, birds are dying from poisoned meat."

They landed near a flock of vultures. Croaking, grunting, hissing and screeching as they fought for best access in this very noisy vulture restaurant.

"This is the best dining, because these dead cows are free of drugs," said Vikram.

Karlha soon ripped into some tasty cow meat. "How do you know?"

"This is a safe zone for us vultures. These are sacred cows, not the farmers' cows."

"I can't smell the difference."

"But I can. And if I show you how to smell the difference, you can learn."

And so Karlha tagged along with Vikram. It was a matter of survival, but after more of these dinner dates, quickly developed into much more. Soon the pair were performing aerial displays, soaring close to each other. Vikram was an expert on the wing. He was very impressed by her incredible journey from Tibet, pressing her for fine details about the mountains and the yaks. Was it really possible to eat everything there, without deadly drugs in the meat?

Karlha swore it was true. It sounded marvellous to Vikram. Karlha set up a challenge. Did Vikram dare to fly over the Himalayas to Tibet, to meet her parents and her griffon clan?

Vikram never backed down from a challenge. In the end, they found a flock of Bar-headed Geese heading back from India to nest in Tibet in the spring, and tagged along with them. Upon returning to Tibet, Karlha and Vikram set up a nest on a niche in the rocks, high on a cliff.

Karlha hatched

a large single egg

And her whole world changed. When that egg hatched, she knew there would be a thousand questions. Like this one: *What lies over the snow-capped mountains?*

Insight

In Tibet, before the Chinese occupation, areas near lakes controlled by the Tibetan government had a rich bird life. The government assigned and paid people to safeguard these birds and their eggs. Environmental protection in those days was not spurred by the kind of preservation awareness we have today. It was rather influenced by the Buddha's teaching of safeguarding the life of all living beings.

—HH Dalai Lama

The Antelope Detective

& the Strange Case of the Missing Wool

A wild and woolly tale from West Tibet, bordering Ladakh

In all his years as a detective, Loden had never seen anything like it. Normally, when Tibetan Antelope relatives and friends reported missing antelopes, it was a case of a wolf attack. Others would get lost on migration and fall over a ravine or something like that. Once there was a very heavy snow storm in winter and some antelopes got confused and perished when they could not find shelter. But what lay in front of him was altogether a different case. There were a dozen antelopes lying on the grass. They were almost certainly the same antelopes reported missing by several family groups.

Loden moved in closer. One by one they had been killed. But why? The bodies seemed to be intact. But then he noticed that they were missing their lower skins, where their underwool should be. That wool is what saves the antelope in freezing conditions of snow and ice in Tibet. The monster that committed this crime was after just one thing: the valuable underwool.

Loden swore he would find those who killed these antelopes in cold blood. But solving this case required some help, which is where Gangze came in. Antelope assistant detective. She had a good nose for trouble. A great sense of direction, rarely got lost. His partner in solving crime. She was a whizz on finding the fine details, and Loden connected all the dots. Between them, they had to crack the case.

They started with tracks of fat tires. It was a human transport, heading south. Loden memorized the pattern of the tires. If they lost the tracks in the mud, they could recognize them later.

There were many obstacles to overcome. Slippery icy ground, snowstorm, freezing cold winds.

And then they made a break-through in the case. Peering around a ridge, they sighted a truck with ten humans—and antelope skins. Followed by the thunder of shooting sticks.

"The humans are trying to kill us!" Loden yelled. "Run!"

They took off at top antelope speed.

The trail led south toward Kashmir, but here the antelopes ran into a big problem. They could not go lower because they knew they would die from the heat. The antelope's coat is terrific in freezing places, keeping it warm and toasty. But this coat cannot be taken off.

With a drop in height, as the temperature and humidity go higher, the antelope would overheat. Which would be deadly.

The antelope detectives thought this over, and decided to give the final task to another animal to report back.

Which animal? They debated for a long time and finally decided on a bird. Which bird? Well, what better spy than a crow? Crows are smart, curious, sharp-eyed, can go anywhere, can land lightly, can get in close.

They found a clever crow, a Himalayan red-billed chough

called Khandro.

"Take a good look at my wool," said Gangze. "That's what we want you to find out about."

"What's in it for me?" asked Khandro.

"You will save us from extinction. Isn't that reward enough? Next they will come for you!"

The crow shook her head. No deal. But Loden got an idea. He told the crow to come back next day at the same spot. Loden asked Gangze: "What does a crow want most in the world?"

Gangze talked to other birds. The thing they crave is a beautiful nest. Red-billed choughs are particular about nests. They build a big nest out of sticks and roots, and then they line the nest with hair—or wool—to make it softer for laying eggs.

Wool! Guess who has the best wool on earth? Tibetan antelopes. Gangze cut a piece of underwool from Loden, and gave it to Khandro.

"This wool keeps us antelopes warm. It will do the same for your eggs." Khandro had never seen such wonderful wool. Lightweight, very warm. She was delighted. Now she could see the importance of keeping antelopes alive. Loden and Gangze promised more wool once the mission was completed.

Khandro set off down the valley. Her mission took a week. The antelopes waited and worried in the foothills, sweating even at these higher altitudes.

Flying over some courtyards in the city of the wool,

Khandro could see the wool of the antelope lying on the ground. They had big machines and were spinning the wool—into a form of clothing.

After long days of observation, Khandro returned to give her report to the antelopes.

"Brace yourselves, I have good news and bad news."

"Tell us the bad news," said Loden.

"You're not going to like this at all. The humans spin and weave the antelope wool into long pieces that can be wrapped around their shoulders. This keeps the humans very warm as they have no fur of their own to protect themselves. The buyers of these wraps are very rich."

Loden could not believe what he was hearing. A transfer of fur. Antelopes are dying so that the humans can stay warm.

"How much antelope wool is needed to make a wrap?" asked Gangze.

"The wool of at least three antelopes," calculated the crow.

"That means those 12 dead antelopes were made into three or four wraps," said Loden, as he whistled.

"Terrible!" said Gangze, her eyes wide. "We must find a way to stop this or we will all be hunted to death!"

"What is the good news? You said there is some good news?"

"Yes. None of this spinning and weaving of antelope

wool is necessary!" said Khandro. "The humans also make the same wraps from the underwool of goats."

"What's the difference?"

"The goats are in herds that the humans protect. They take the underwool, called cashmere. The humans cut off the wool in the summer, when the goats do not need it."

"That would never work for antelopes," said Loden. "We love our freedom too much to be controlled by humans."

Loden turned this over. *So the goat underwool does the same job as antelope underwool. Not as good, not as fine, but still does the job. Problem solved, case closed,* thought Loden.

But he knew in his heart that humans would not settle for goat underwool when there was finer wool to be found from antelopes.

"The real problem," Gangze said, echoing his thoughts, "is human greed. Antelopes get along fine with no possessions, but humans must gather all kinds of things. Things they do not even need."

With this new knowledge, and heavy hearts, Gangze and Loden turned north—heading home to Tibet. But every problem has a solution. They knew it would take time—and they were determined to find that solution to enable antelopes to survive. Heavy hearts, but heads held high—as they struggled up a steep mountain pass to cross into Tibet.

SOLUTION

In the year 2000, the trade in Tibetan Antelope underwool was banned in Kashmir, the main centre for weaving of the wool. 'The Real Antelope Detectives' at the back of this book (with the Tibetan Antelope profile) gives more details. Shipments of shawls were seized around the world. Fine cashmere wool (*pashmina*) from domestic goats makes excellent shawls and should be used instead of antelope underwool.

Insight

Killing animals for sport, for pleasure, for adventure, and for hides and furs is a phenomenon which is at once disgusting and distressing. There is no justification in indulging in such acts of brutality.

—HH Dalai Lama

Life is as dear to a mute creature as it is to a man. Just as one wants happiness and fears pain, just as one wants to live and not to die, so do other creatures.

—HH Dalai Lama

The Angry Bear

Barno the radical Tibetan Brown Bear: a story with claws—one that will give you paws...

Western Sichuan

I am running full tilt through the forest. There are a dozen dogs in hot pursuit, chasing me, barking furiously. Humans are urging them on. What did I ever do to humans? Why are they hunting me down? I know the dogs cannot climb a tree, so that could be an escape route. But I know the humans are clever and will find a way of trapping me, even in a tree.

Bears like me have a few tricks up our sleeves. I know the caves here like the back of my hand. I dodge into a cave complex and stand up hidden by a wall. The dogs are confused. They mill around at the entrance, but cannot see anything in the cave—it's too dark. The humans do not have lights. One human steps into the cave and I let out a strange roar. He jumps back, spooked, and quickly exits the cave.

Barno wakes up in a sweat, eyes wide open in fear. He takes in his surroundings. He is in a cave—no dream there. It's the end of winter, and as the last snows recede high in the mountains, Himalayan bears wake up from their long sleep in caves. Four months long.

They are very very hungry, and in the case of Barno, very cranky as well.

Barno is prone to recurring nightmares, but he has positive dreams too. He dreams big. He dreams about solutions to the terrible treatment of his brothers and sisters at the hands of humans in China. He dreams of Freedom for all bears.

Freedom from zoos. Freedom from farms where bears are held captive for medicine extraction. Liberation! Dreams of setting up the Bear Liberation Front, to free all captive bears from their misery, no matter what species of bear.

Barno is mad at humans. Can you blame him? For years he was held in a tiny cage and milked for bile, a trade that is vile. The bile is used for Traditional Chinese Medicine. How sick is that? Actually, it gets worse—much worse. Bear-paw soup is supposed to make humans as strong as a bear. *Nonsense!*

Humans have taken everything from bears. They are super-predators, with greed out of control.

Barno's big break came when his keeper got drunk and left a latch loose. Barno's claws did the rest, releasing the latch and making good time at midnight through the forest, getting as far away as he could. Feasting on delicious berries along the way, chasing some deer.

A few days later, by chance, Barno crosses tracks with his old paramour, Wangmo. But is shocked to learn she has two cubs now, paired up with a rival bear.

"You were gone for five years, Barno. I thought you were dead. Don't look at me like that. It's not my fault!"

Barno wanders back into the forest and with a great

howling sound, smashes every tree he can find with his bear hands. He is hopping mad. He is foaming at the mouth. He is mad as Hell. He is fighting mad. That night he steals a case of beer from a hut, rips open the cans with his claws, and drinks the lot. Then he picks a fight with another bear.

"Hey, what's your problem?" shouts the other bear. "Is this about territory?"

"No, not about territory. My problem is that I am mad as a hornet."

Mad as a hornet? Wait a minute. That sparks a great idea. *Don't get mad. Get even.*

It's the fault of the humans. They have robbed him of his freedom for five years. They have taken away his life—and his wife. And Barno is going to settle the score. After his miraculous escape, Barno sets about trashing villages when the humans are off working in the fields.

But there are some other bears who get along very well with humans. Like the Giant Panda. Deep in the bamboo forest of western Sichuan, Barno meets a Giant Panda with black-and white markings and black mask over his eyes.

Xi-Xi is his name. He is named after the President, whom he actually resembles. Barno knows that Giant Pandas are well-treated by humans, but not the reasons why, so he asks Xi-Xi how come Pandas get respectful treatment. The Panda deliberates for some time.

"We pandas were once much-feared and hunted down,

same as you. Then we were noticed by a foreign wildlife society and slowly became the symbol of China. And we became world-famous."

"You become world-famous while we are kept in cages and treated terribly. How did that happen?" asks Barno.

"Here's how it works," explains Xi-Xi, chewing on a piece of bamboo. "Everybody loves cute cuddly pandas. So China rents them out to zoos in foreign places. And if that nation upsets China, or does something naughty, they take the panda back.

Panda Diplomacy, it is called—or Panda blackmail."

"So you have become a cute toy! How can you even call yourself a bear? You know what, Xi-Xi, you are just a white bear with a few fancy black spots. A white bear with two black eyes. You're an embarrassment to the entire bear race."

"Haha! Precisely! You got it right on target, you old brown bear. Of course we are an embarrassment! A group of us is called an Embarrassment of Pandas."

The Panda starts dancing around, shouting:

a parliament of owls, a dazzle of zebras, a pride of lions, a gaggle of geese, a kettle of vultures, a murder of crows, a pandemonium of parrots, a troop of monkeys, a school of fish, a leap of leopards, and— an embarrassment of pandas

The one thing that Barno learns from the Giant Panda is that the tables can be turned on humans. So how to develop a healthy respect for all bears? Barno thinks it over. Barno loves pranks. Pranks with a purpose. To spook humans. Barno can terrify humans by preying on their imagination for mythical beasts.

Barno gets a brilliant idea from a comic book left behind by humans. Can't follow the strange language, but can follow the drawings. There is a tall strange mountain creature that scares the heck out of humans. The creature looks almost like Barno, but it has white hair and it walks upright on two legs. And it leaves giant footprints in the snow. One night, Barno rolls in the snow, covering himself in a layer of white stuff. He has turned into the much-feared Yeti—the Snowman of Tibet. He rushes past some workers in the forest, making howling sounds. The workers run off, screaming.

One of the workers has dropped a bag. Barno opens the bag. His eyes light up. Inside is a large key. He knows what that key is immediately. How he hated that key.

The same key that kept him in a cage all those years.

And now Barno is turning things over, thinking about how to get even.

Time to turn the tables. Barno teams up with like-minded bears, and they make plans. Big plans. He goes over the ideas with his bear pals, Jigme and Wangdu.

"So Jigme, you love honey, right?"

"Sure thing."

"And you know how mad those bees get when you steal their hive?"

"Oh yeah! Tell me about it! They go nuts!"

"Well, we are going to put that anger to good use."

"How?"

"You steal the hive and we drop it in the human camp. Then they will attack the humans."

"That's brilliant, Barno!"

"A bear with bees in his bonnet."

The target is a bear-bile farm. He shows the bears the key to the cages. There is only one key, but Barno knows the locks are the same for all the cages. He trains the bears how to open the cages. They will go in an hour before dawn and start opening the cages, before the workers wake up. The bears high-five with their paws at midnight, and send a chilling roar into the night air.

Just before dawn, Jigme and Wangdu advance with stolen bee hives, and scores of mad bees behind them. Covered in snow, Barno and other bears that look like the much-feared

Yeti follow. They start unlocking the cages.

Awakened by odd noises, the sleepy and confused human workers stumble out of their huts, swarmed by bees, who sting them. And spooked by Yetis, who howl at them. The workers mill around in confusion, desperately trying to escape the stinging bees and the howling Yetis. Some jump into a nearby lake to hide. Others are pursued into the forest. And Barno and his fellow bears get to work, unlocking the latch of each bear cage.

Dozens of bears emerge into the chilly morning air. They quickly head for the forest, sniffing the fresh scents, celebrating their freedom. Smelling the trees, the berries, the animals of the forest. Sharpening their claws on tree trunks. Rolling around on the ground. *Bears will never be oppressed!* They roar. *Victory to the bears!*

SOLUTION

The medicine made from bear-bile is not proven effective. In any case, the active ingredient, known as ursodiol, can be made in a lab, so no need to get it from live bears.

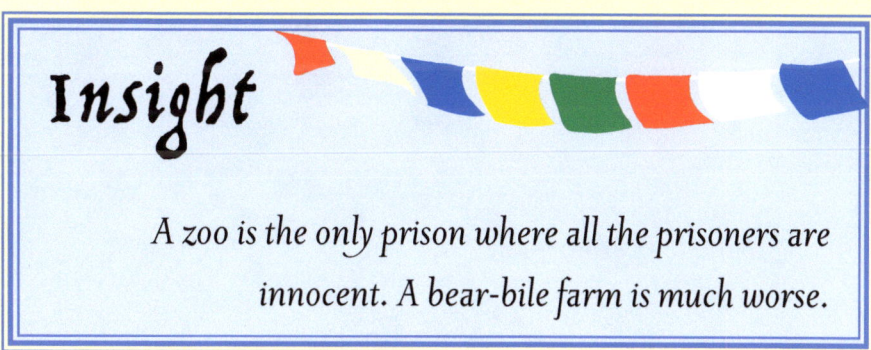

Insight

A zoo is the only prison where all the prisoners are innocent. A bear-bile farm is much worse.

The Big-Hearted Takin

Kinley the Takin is on a mission to save all animals, not just his own kin— or his own skin

Pemako, Yarlung Tsangpo river valley, east Tibet

Wolf attack! You know the drill! Big males to stand rear guard and keep the wolves away, while females and young head for the hills. Kinley is the biggest male of all, with the biggest nose, the biggest horns—and the biggest heart. There are several wolves hanging around. And they have their eyes on more than the Takins.

There is a Blue Sheep nearby. Kinley rushes over and gives a wolf a good kick. The wolf yelps and turns and runs, causing the other wolves to run off too.

"That sheep is not one of ours! Leave him!" shouts Marmuk.

"Listen, he is from the same family as us. He is our brother. All life is precious! We must help him too."

"Kinley, you cannot help all the animals! You must look out for your own kind first."

Kinley and Marmuk are friends, but unusual friends, because they disagree on just about everything. They seem to enjoy disagreeing. In fact, whenever Kinley gives Marmuk any advice, he will go and do the exact opposite.

They even butt horns over their differences.

Kinley counters:

"Oh I disagree with you there. We must save our brothers and sisters too—the antelopes, goats and deer."

"Deer? when did you ever save a deer?"

"Three months ago. It was a Musk Deer—a deer with a funny face with two fangs. But despite the fangs, it was unable to defend itself against a wolf."

Pemako, the Lotus-land, is a beautiful valley with lots of forest and green ferns and shrubs, and gushing rivers, cascading waterfalls and towering snowy peaks. It is beautiful, but the valley is changing, right before the eyes of the Takins.

As time goes on, more humans are moving into the valley, cutting down trees—taking away the food and the home of the Takins. And that means a lot more animal casualties.

Kinley moves to warn all animals living in trees. A big tree comes crashing down. A mother bird in a nest is dead, but her chicks survive. How to help? Wait until a shocked father bird returns. He will have to raise the chicks now.

The same humans cutting down trees are going after big animals—for a very strange reason. Kinley peers into a human house through a window and is shocked to see animal heads

on the wall. It is time to leave. The Takins need to get out of this place.

A promising way out comes from a chance encounter. Out searching for food one day, Kinley bumps into a Himalayan Tahr, with a big shock of hair.

"Kinley, don't you remember me?" Kinley looks puzzled.

"You rescued me from a wolf when I was small."

"Tara! How big you have grown, so much hair! That's why I didn't recognise you."

And that, Tara explains, is her biggest problem: she wishes she didn't have so much hair. The heat in these valleys is getting too much. The Himalayan Tahr is a huge goat, with a huge coat of hair—and cannot remove the hair when overheating. She is thinking about moving to a higher, colder place.

"And where would that be?"

"Across the border, in Bhutan. I know the way."

Tara talks about her dream of getting to Bhutan. No tree cutting, no animal hunting. Much cooler. Respect for trees, respect for animals.

"In fact, Takins get the most respect."

"Why is that?"

"You are the national animal. So the highest respect and well-protected. There is a legend about the origin of the Takin."

"What is the story?"

"Many years ago, a mad yogi was asked by his followers to perform a miracle, so he took a goat, an antelope and a cow and mixed them together to make a Takin."

Kinley turns to Marmuk.

"Ah, you see Marmuk, you made a mistake. We are not one animal! We are a miraculous mix. And that's why I save our cousins—the goats and the antelopes and the deer."

After chatting with Tara, the Takins come together to talk about the future. There are around 50 of them in the group—males, females and young. They decide the future is not so good for the young in Pemako. The future sounds much brighter in Bhutan. Even Marmuk agrees with this decision.

After working out with Tara which direction to take, the Takin trail builders set to work, clearing a trail to the south, toward Bhutan. Well, making Takin tunnels through the foliage. Takins do not follow human trails. Tara is thrilled to join them. Their march toward Bhutan is delayed by a few days after the discovery of a salt lick. All the Takins fight over the best positions to get at the salt. Males butt heads—they are fighting over salt. Why do Takins love salt? Nobody knows. But they get excited about salt, that's for sure. They finally resume the long walk to Bhutan.

The group runs into obstacles—at one point, they have to climb a steep rock wall. They can handle all this, but they come up against one obstacle that has them confused. It is a very fast river, with rocks in the middle. The Takins size it up. They decide it is too risky to swim across. The river is too fast and too dangerous. But there is an old bridge made from iron chains. It sways horribly. All the Takins are terrified. One of them starts to cross, but the bridge wobbles and the Takin turns back. Then Tara steps forward. For some reason, Tara is not afraid. She shimmies across the bridge in short order, and waves from the other side. See, it's possible.

Fancy footwork! The Takins are green with envy.

Tara and Kinley have to reassure the Takins to cross, one by one. The bridge is very shaky, and it wobbles a lot, making it hard to stand up. One mis-step could mean slipping—and falling into the river far below. The bridge is made for humans, not Takins. But slowly, carefully, each Takin makes the crossing on the iron-chain bridge.

Finally the Takins march over a high pass into Bhutan. A few more days of hoofing it brings them down to a forest paradise. Lush things to feed on—so many trees, shrubs, bushes, grasses and herbs. Forest as far as the eye can see. Chirping of birds in the trees. New sounds, birds they have never heard before.

Beautiful flowers. They marvel at blue poppies. This is like seeing the world with new eyes. They have made the right choice. All their hardship has been worth it.

Then Kinley gets the biggest shock of his life. An intense stare from a strange orange animal with black stripes. This unknown striped animal is not eating grass. It is looking at the Takins with a steely stare.

"Veg or non-veg?"

"Definitely non-veg. Look at those teeth and claws."

"Maybe we can outrun it?"

"I don't think so. Look at those strong legs."

How to defend against an unknown animal attack? This animal probably does not know much about Takins either, so the element of surprise is the best way to go. The Takins decide to strike first.

The Takins make a fearsome sight with a long row of horns. They attack with muffled roars. The strange orange animal with the black stripes rushes away at top speed.

Soon after, the Takins meet some of their Bhutan cousins. Bhutan Takins have a funny accent, quite different from Kinley's group, who are Mishmi Takins from Tibet. "Welcome to Bhutan!" The Bhutan Takins want to hear all about the long journey from Tibet. Kinley brings up the subject of the unknown animal.

"So what is the orange beast with black stripes?"

"Ah yes, that is called a Tiger and it will eat you for breakfast if you don't watch out. But not common in the highlands, mostly lowlands. Lately it has been getting hotter and Tigers are moving higher."

"And what is the defence against this animal?" asks Kinley. "Climb a cliff. The Tiger has paws that are good for running, but no use for climbing a cliff."

As they are speaking, some humans walk past in the distance. "Run for cover!" shouts Marmuk.

"Relax, just stay where you are," says a Bhutan Takin. "The humans will not hurt you here. They leave you alone. You are in a park. It's different from Tibet. In Bhutan, you are the national animal. Remember that—and walk with your head held high!"

Bhutan is looking just like the promised land. Tara is delighted. It is everything she dreamed of. Well, except for the Tiger. As Kinley is standing up on his back legs to munch on some tree branches, he notices a large bee, buzzing in a spider-web. The largest bee that Kinley has ever seen, and about to come to a sticky end as lunch for a spider. Kinley is going to change that. He sets about freeing the bee from the spider-web.

"Kinley, why do you want to rescue that creature? It will only sting you," says Marmuk.

"No, you've got it all wrong," says Kinley. "This is the most important creature on earth—working every day for all of us."

"What do you mean?"

"No bees, no flowers, no fruit. No green. No berries, no food for you and me. There is no creature on earth that works so hard for us. You see those beautiful blue poppies? They do not grow without bees."

This is Kinley's first rescue in Bhutan.

"But you can't save all the bees!" says Marmuk.

"No," says Kinley beaming. "But I can save this one!"

Kinley takes part of the spider-web into his horns and shakes it to the ground. The exhausted bee struggles free from the web. It takes one look at the eyes of Kinley,

breaks into a huge smile

and buzzes off into the forest, heading back home.

Insight

On this planet, there are billions of insects, animals and plants. We humans need all of them— we cannot survive alone. Since all living things on Earth are interdependent, we have to act to protect the environment as a matter of our own survival and happiness.

—HH Gyalwang Karmapa

If the bee disappeared off the surface of the globe then man would only have four years of life left. No more bees, no more pollination, no more plants, no more animals, no more man.

—quote attributed to Albert Einstein

Songs of The Wild Yak

Rogtur the wacky Wild Yak loves singing, and he loves Yanglha—so why not sing his way into her heart?

Valley of the Wild Yaks, Amdo, northeast Tibet

Rogtur is standing in the ice-cold river, cooling his heels—or rather, his hooves. It's close to sunset, and as beautiful light hits the snow mountains and turns them pink, he loves to sing.

The sun is shining, the sky is blue—

but under the humans the environment is not true

The Wild Yaks of this region are famous for their singing. Two out of three of them are singers or poets, or planning to become one or the other.

Why is Rogtur standing in the ice-cold river? Because he is too hot in his long shaggy coat. And it's all the fault of the humans. Rogtur sounds off with a longer song:

It's all your fault that I am too hot in my woolly winter coat that I cannot take off: I am so used to life in the snow that now I have absolutely nowhere to go

It's all your fault there are so many fences that grass is disappearing

before our senses: you dig deeper and deeper in the ground—
—but we have no idea what you have found

I'm not the only one with a thick woolly coat: the antelopes are far too hot, and the goats, and the Blue Sheep, the Marmots and the Bears
—all moving higher and higher, but who cares?

Standing in the ice-cold water nearby is Rogtur's best friend Dhongkar, who listens and grunts approval at times.

Dhongkar is named after a big white patch on his forehead. Dhongkar is known among his herd as the Joker. He loves to crack jokes. He will never be a poet or a singer, but he is the best stand-up Joker of the herd. Changing the subject, Dhongkar jokes about his plans for the weekend: mainly butting heads and locking horns with other males, and snorting a lot to impress the females.

"What about you?" he asks Rogtur.

"Ah, planning to go further afield," says Rogtur. "I've got a date. Can you keep a secret?"

Dhongkar's ears stand up. "I'm all ears."

"She's not from our herd."

"Whose herd then?"

"A herd with the bells around their necks."

"Are you crazy? That's a herd run by humans. That's very dangerous, Rogtur."

"Yes, but I have the perfect plan."

Rogtur goes to see his fellow grass-eaters at the Kyang herd—Tibetan wild donkeys. Frisky Kyangs are rolling in the dust. They love rolling in the dust. Rogtur asks them why. The

Kyangs respond: no idea. In return, they ask Rogtur: why do yaks grunt? Good question! Well, they grunt when they are worried, or courting. Wild Yaks grunt in mating season, and that's why Rogtur is asking the Kyangs for help. Rogtur has his eyes on Yanglha, a pretty young nak with long brown hair and lighter undercoat. Nak? Is that a mistake? No, that's the female yak. She came into the area with a human caravan—all the yaks loaded with yak-hair bags and tents that the humans move around with. The yak-herders milk the yaks and make their food. The minute Rogtur saw Yanglha in the caravan, he knew he had to get closer. One day, he managed to get close toward nightfall and found out her name. She found out his name too. They exchanged grunts.

And now, with the help of the Kyangs, he can get closer. He can hide among the Kyang herd to get closer to the herders' camp. He can hear the booming sound of bells attached to the yaks, around their necks. Yanglha is eating grass when the enchanting song floats through the air in perfect yak dialect. But Kyangs do not speak this dialect, so where is this coming from?

She catches sight of Rogtur among the herd of Kyangs. Such a handsome young yak! Such magnificent horns! They lock eyes. Her heart melts as she listens to the song...

I love your hairy brown face and your horns—and your grace—
the way your skirt falls to the ground, the way you grunt—that
*sweet sound—and I feel—*Rogtur's song is cut short by a fierce

herder's dog, the Tibetan Mastiff. The huge hairy dog comes running toward him, barking loudly. You can fool the humans, but not the guard dog.

The guard dog is all teeth, and it looks ferocious. Rogtur moves back into the middle of the Kyang herd, which confuses the dog. Where did that yak go? The herders have now spotted Rogtur and start throwing rocks at him, using yak-hair slings. Those herders—they make everything from yaks, even weapons.

Rogtur never realized how dangerous this encounter would be: attacked by a huge dog, having stones thrown at him by herders.

And then back with his own herd, some strong words from the other Wild Yaks: leave that kind of yak alone, she is nothing but trouble. She is from the wrong side of the tracks. They refer to the human-made tracks, where big transports hurtle by.

Rogtur stalks off, in a bad mood with his tail up in the air. He goes to talk with Dhongkar. "You know, us Wild Yaks are in a time of crisis. Long ago, my grandfather told me that we roamed freely, went wherever we wanted, did as we pleased.

And the humans left us alone. What does it mean to be a Wild Yak today? Hunted, pushed off the good grass, desert sand advancing, humans digging up the grasslands all over the place—putting up fences, making a big mess."

"And polluting the rivers," adds Dhongkar. "Remember the day we almost lost Kargyan?"

"Oh yes, how could I ever forget that? The day we found her collapsed on the banks of the river, very sick. All she did was drink water. But in that small river, dead fish were floating along. Whatever the humans put into that river killed the fish—and nearly killed Kargyan."

Rogtur tries to keep Yanglha out of his mind, thinking it is hopeless to chase her. But a few days later, that changes in a rather startling way. A Ruddy Shelduck flies in, out of breath but honking loudly. This exhausted bird brings an urgent message about two yaks separated, and some herders taking them down a trail.

That can only mean one thing: they are going to the market. The yaks will be sold. And that could be the end of their lives. Rogtur finds out that one of the yaks, with a brown coat, must be Yanglha. He must act quickly. Following the Ruddy Shelduck, honking loudly, Rogtur and Dhongkar thunder over the grasslands and race to the head of the trail. They must block the humans so Yanglha can escape.

Yak attack! A Wild Yak can be twice the size of a herder yak. The herders are spooked. And they do not have their ferocious dog with them. They try to pick up some stones, but Rogtur and Dhongkar charge with huge horns pointed at them. The herders scream and jump off the trail—and run for the hills.

Yanglha runs down the trail.

"My heart is beating so fast!" says Yanglha.

"From love?" asks Dhongkar.

"No, you idiot! From our close escape!"

"Yanglha, you cannot go back with the herders now," says Rogtur. "They will take you to the market. You must stay with us. We will take care of you."

"You don't have to convince me, Rogtur! I know what the market means. I have no wish to go back. I like my freedom!" Dhongkar jokes that Rogtur has a musical girlfriend, with a bell around her neck. The singer and the music.

"You should call her Tinkerbell."

"That is not funny, my friend! Not funny at all," shouts Rogtur.

Dhongkar has drawn attention to the bell, and it seems to Rogtur that Yanglha's bell has to go, or the herders will be able to find her. They must take the bell off. But how? It is held around Yanglha's neck with a rope made from yak-hair. Yaks have teeth made for eating grass, not for cutting anything. They have no upper teeth, only hard gums. So who has the sharp teeth? A light goes on in Rogtur's head. The Kyangs! Both upper and lower teeth so they can bite and fight. Yaks use their horns to fight. Kyangs use their teeth to fight.

With the help of some sharp Kyang teeth, the rope around Yanglha's neck is shredded. The bell falls to the ground.

"I am finally free!" exclaims Yanglha.

"You are now a Wild Yak!" says Rogtur. Night has fallen. Under the canopy of a million stars, Rogtur breaks into song:

These grasslands are our lands—
endless blue sky and desert sands—
from the Great Blue Lake to the northeast
to the Mighty Forests of the southeast,
from the Big Open Wilderness in the north
to the Snowy Mountains in the south,
As far as the yak's eye can see,
These grasslands belong to you and me—
It was fate that I met you by chance—
Yanglha, may I have this first dance?

"The dance of freedom, yes!"

Insight

If animals could speak, mankind would weep.
—Anthony Douglas Williams

Crazy Old Sand Fox

Zinon the Sand Fox compares notes with Yeshey the Eagle-owl on why their world keeps changing and going darker...

Sanjiangyuan National Park, Amdo, northeast Tibet

It's hard to hide in high desert. No trees to hide behind, only bushes. But Zinon knows all the tricks. Zinon's yellowish-grey coat is perfect for blending into the landscape. Stay still like a rock. Keep low on the ground. Move in slow motion.

Wait for the right time. Be very sneaky.

Times are good for the Tibetan Sand Fox. So much desert. Maybe too much desert. More and more desert each year. But life needs grass and shrubs to keep going here.

How can a large animal survive in a semi-desert? The short answer is: Pikas, or rock-rabbits. These animals dig holes in the ground to live in. They eat bushes and grasses, and a bunch of predators hunt them. Bears, eagles, wolves, Pallas' Cats and Sand Foxes all eat them, because they are so common. They hunt other prey, like the Woolly Hare and the Himalayan Marmot, but it is easier to hunt Pikas.

Toward the end of winter, Zinon has a weird day that

changes everything. It all starts with a dead eagle.

The eagle has dined on the same food as Zinon does: the eagle has eaten a Pika. How does Zinon know this? Because he can smell the poison the humans feed to the Pikas. Trick or treat? Zinon lost half his family to poisoned Pikas. He lost his partner and daughter. His son survived—now grown up and moved away to start his own family. His son survived because Zinon taught him how to smell the poison.

The shrill whistle of Pikas alerts others to the arrival of the Sand Fox. They all dart into their holes. Zinon tries to work out, does he have a bad memory or are those Pikas moving to higher ground? He doesn't remember them being so high up.

Then he finds some easy lunch. A Tibetan Brown Bear has shown up. All Zinon has to do is follow the bear around as he digs up Pika holes. Zinon can catch the Pikas fleeing from the bear. Easy work. But there is something wrong here. Winter is not over, so why is this bear walking around? Should still be asleep in its cave for the winter. Zinon follows the bear for a long distance, going into new territory. Zinon and the bear finally part company. Zinon walks on, but the Pikas are elusive. He walks further and further, much further than his usual range. Towards sunset, he does a double-take.

Can it be? Impossible! Out of the corner of his eye, in the semi-darkness, he spots a black fox!

He has never seen anything like it. The sun is going down, but Zinon is sure the fox is black, not red. The Red Fox comes out around this time to hunt Pikas at night. Foxes in this region are either yellowish or red, never black.

Distracted by this, Zinon is not paying attention and steps on a piece of wood that collapses. He falls right down a deep hole. Now he is in big trouble. He looks around and finds lights in the hole. It is a long tunnel, built by humans. Lots of black rock in the tunnel. Zinon hides in the shadows as some humans pass through. How will he ever escape? There must be a way. He sneezes from the black dust. *Shhhh!* Got to stay silent, like a shadow. The humans are taking the black rock and putting it in bins. Lots of bins. The tunnel is very black and dusty. Why are the humans taking out the black rock?

Zinon has a sleepless night, tossing and turning, and dreaming of black foxes. It takes Zinon hours and hours to work out that the bins of black rock are going outside, and he must hide in a bin to reach the outside. He finally gets the courage to get into a bin, along with the black rock—and he is right. The bin travels somehow to the surface, back into the daylight, next morning. He jumps out of the bin and runs off across the grasslands as fast as his legs will take him.

Later that morning, out hunting Pikas, he finds he has competition—from Lhakpa, the young Tibetan Wolf, with a sleek grey coat and some yellowish patterns, but not nearly as good for blending in as the Sand Fox coat, he tells himself.

But Lhakpa is certainly faster than him on the chase.

Zinon tells Lhakpa the tale of the dead eagle, the wide-awake bear and the black fox. Know-it-all young Lhakpa looks at Zinon with a glint in her eyes: "Let's face it, Zinon, you're too old for this. You're losing your marbles, you crazy old Sand Fox! Get a grip! Black fox, no such thing! Ha ha!"

Determined to find answers to these riddles, Zinon decides to visit Chimi the Pallas' Cat, in her cave. Chimi is a sort of mini Snow Leopard—much smaller than Zinon, but fierce, with sharp claws, and very grumpy. The grumpiest cat in the world. But don't mistake this for a kitty. Like the Snow Leopard and the big cats, Chimi has round circles at the centre of her eyes, not slits. Zinon tells Chimi about the dead eagle and the wide-awake bear. Chimi takes it all in stride, but at the mention of the black fox, she suddenly flares up. She looks at Zinon oddly and snarls: "You're bats! Nuts! Bananas! No such animal! Cuckoo! Hare-brained!"

Zinon walks away with his tail tucked between his legs. Has he just imagined all this?

Oohu-oohu-oohu!

A deep hooting noise alerts Zinon to the presence of Yeshey, the Eurasian Eagle-owl. But where is he? Zinon looks around. Nothing.

Oohu-oohu-oohu! Getting closer. Blending in so well that even Zinon cannot see him. Yeshey's eyes are closed. Once they open, Zinon can see the large pumpkin-orange eyes of this huge owl, which is half-eagle and can take down large prey.

Yeshey is sitting on a shrub, and spins his head in the direction

of Zinon.

"Yeshey my friend, strange things have been happening lately."

"Yah, tell me about it." Zinon starts with the dead eagle.

"Poison," says Yeshey. "Humans poison them. No idea why. Bad for all of us."

Zinon mentions Pikas moving to higher ground.

"Too hot," says Yeshey. "They can't take the heat so they are moving higher."

Zinon talks about the Tibetan Brown Bear.

"Too hot," says Yeshey. "Can't do the long winter sleep anymore. Waking up from the long sleep much earlier."

Hmm. So far, so good, thinks Zinon. Now to drop the big

news. "I saw a black fox, toward sunset."

Yeshey stares at him for a while. "Oh yes, I have seen it too," he says.

"You saw it?!"

"Yes, it lives near the place where the humans dig for black rocks. Lots of black dust goes up in the air, and it lands on the snow—and on the foxes there."

"So it is a Red Fox, really?"

"Exactly, a Red Fox covered with fine black dust. Or half-black, half-red. You just saw one. I have seen several black foxes. Some have black faces and backs, but other parts are still red. More like red-and-black foxes."

Zinon grins. He is not losing his marbles at all. He has a sharper mind than the Tibetan Wolf or the Pallas' Cat. He has out-foxed them!

"How do you know all this stuff, Yeshey?"

"You see these wings, my friend?" Yeshey displays his impressive wingspan—which is longer than Zinon's entire body.

"I spend half my life up in the air," says Yeshey, "covering great distances, gliding on my wings. My eyes are very sharp. I can see for long distances. I see everything. Nothing escapes me. And to find prey, I have to pay attention to tiny details. It's like I have eyes in the back of my head."

Yeshey swivels his head all the way around, left and right, to show that nothing can escape those eyes.

"The black rock—why do the humans dig for it?" asks Zinon.

"They store it and burn it in winter to stay warm. You have your very warm hairy coat and I have my very warm feathers. I even have feathers on my feet to keep me warm. But the humans have nothing, no fur or feathers, so they burn the black rock. Going black gives the Red Fox an advantage for hunting toward night. It is a black animal hunting in darkness. Except for one thing."

"What's that?"

"The Pikas are turning black from the dust as well. Hard to hunt at night when Pikas are blacker. A black fox trying to hunt black Pikas in complete darkness. Tough for me, as well. I hunt at night. Everything is turning black. The grass and bushes are turning black. The sand is turning black."

Zinon turns over this shocking new information for some time.

"Where does this end?" Zinon asks.

Yeshey bobs his head up and down and around, considering his answer carefully:

"Burning the black rock changes the air—it means the heat is rising, and that's why the Pikas are moving higher. And where the Pikas go, you and I, and the bears and the wolves must go."

Zinon whistles and shakes his head, and says:

"But the higher we go, the less grass and bushes—and Pikas

need to eat. The desert is growing bigger and bigger. If Pikas go too high, there will be nothing for them to eat."

"Exactly! You got it!"

Zinon is stunned. So many bad things happening at the same time. "What can we do about all this?"

"We must find a different path," says Yeshey. "We must find a way to convince the humans to change their ways. Before we all disappear. And the first step is protest."

"We have no power."

"That is where you are wrong. Nobody is too small. If we work together, we can do some damage of our own. Let me show you something."

Yeshey leads Zinon to a hill with a vast view.

"You see there in the distance?" says Yeshey, flapping his wings. Zinon squints: he can just make out a white human transport, or actually, half-white.

"Last night we birds—the eagles, the owls and the others—flew over in a big flock in the darkness and dropped our loads on the human transports."

"You mean you—"

"Let everything out. It's quite poisonous. Bad for human health—and for their gear. They turn us black, so we turn them white. And on the ground, the Red Foxes go out at night and cut through wires under the transports with their teeth. Then the transports do not work for a week.

Here's the thing—the male foxes are mad about their coats

turning black. They are proud of their reddish brown coats, which attracts female foxes. Females turn their noses up at black coats."

Zinon laughs. It is the first time he has laughed in weeks. He never thought he could laugh in such a bad situation, but here he is, howling with laughter. *This is no laughing matter*, the look on Yeshey's face tells him.

Insight

EARTH *provides enough to satisfy every man's need, but not for every man's* **GREED**.
—Mahatma Gandhi

If you talk to animals,
They will talk with you
and you will know each other.
If you do not talk with them,
You will not know them—
and what you do not know, you will fear.
What one fears, one destroys.
—Chief Dan George

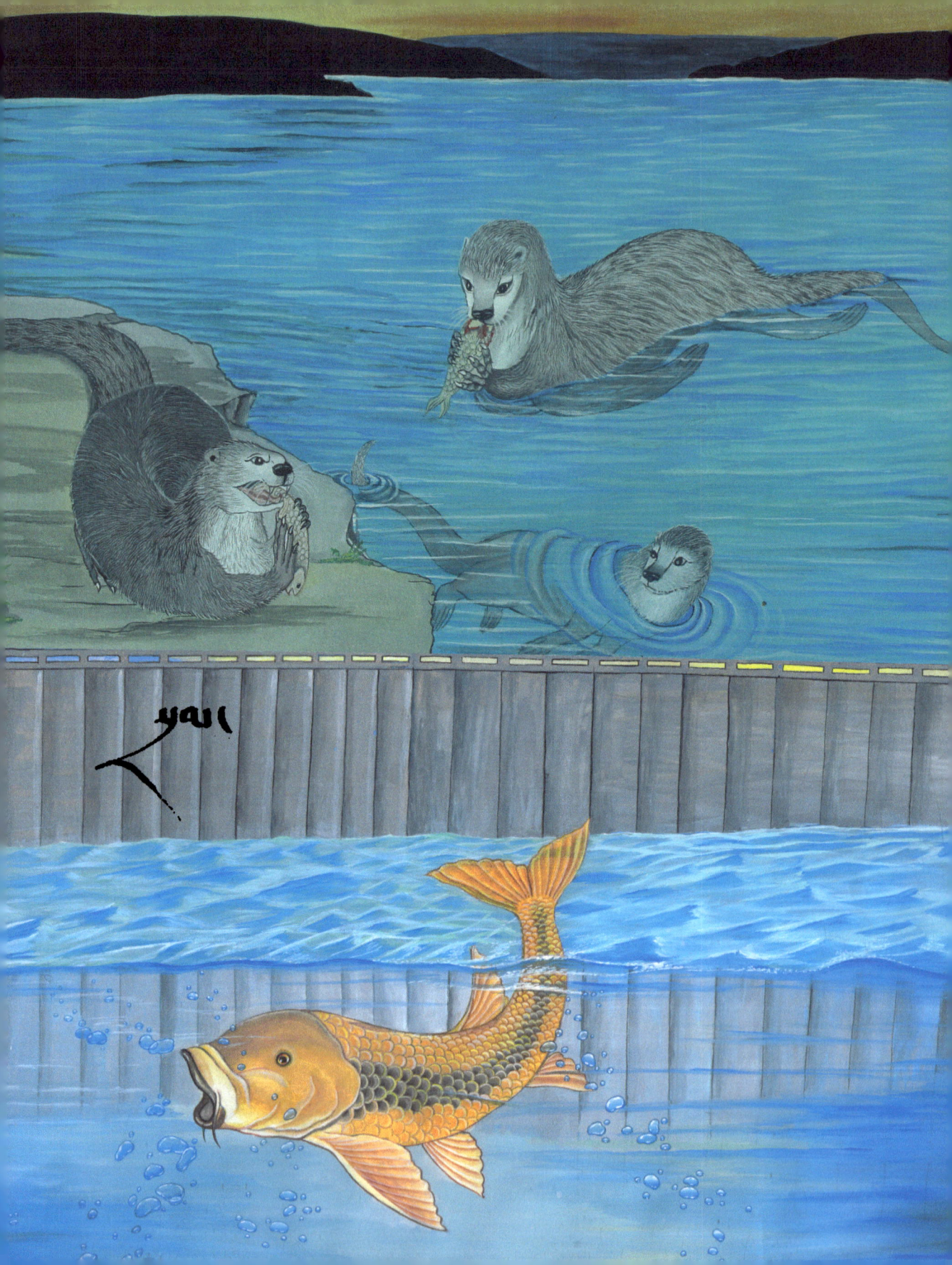

The Unexpected Otter

Lumo the Smooth-coated Otter is swept off her feet
—in more ways than one...

Karnali River, Nepal

One day, along comes a problem that makes you completely forget about all your other problems. A problem so big, the other problems become tiny and disappear. The problems that appear to be droplets of water—and then along comes a raging river of water. And then it all comes down to one big problem: survival. For Lumo the Otter, that day arrived when humans started changing her river. The river she calls home. The otters' home is a nest in the roots of a tree at the river bank, a convenient place to go fishing from. There are four in the family—Lumo, her older brother Nanda, and mother and father.

The problem is a wall, a huge wall across the river that the humans are building, with machinery coming closer and closer to the home of the otters. The BULL dozers, CATERPILLAR tractors, construction CRANES, stone crushers, machines that remove sand from the river. Great noise and dust and commotion. And no fish for supper.

Then one afternoon, when Dad and Nanda are off fishing, a

flash flood comes out of the wall and down the river. Lumo and her mother are swept away in a torrent of water, fighting for their lives.

Argggghhh! topsy-turvy whoosh! sploooosh! water everywhere, can't breathe, bang on rock Ouch! crack, thwack! grab out, no hold, roaring water, crashing rapids, slimy rocks…

They finally wash up on a beach, exhausted, very hungry. Too tired to catch food. It is getting dark. They fall asleep on the beach, hungry and afraid. What has happened to Nanda and Dad? Are they still alive?

The next morning, Lumo's mother discovers she has injured her front paws on rocks in the rapids worse than she thought. Sore, bruised, cut and aching. She quickly realises she cannot catch fish. Their roles are reversed. Lumo must save her mother, but how? She doesn't know how to catch fish.

"My little Lumo, here's what you have to do. You need to grow up very fast—and find us some fish. It's the only way we can survive."

"Who is going to teach me?"

"I can try. You know who taught me how to fish?"

"Your mother?"

"No, humans did. But I was not allowed to eat the fish. We were captured in Bangladesh. The humans used us to catch fish—but they took them from us. One day, I sneaked away, eating all the fish I wanted. And went a long way up the river, starting a new family here. And now we have lost our home and have to start all over again."

Suddenly her mother's eyes go wide, with a look of horror—as a huge eagle swoops in and grabs Lumo in its claws. Instantly, transported way up in the air, flying upriver. Wonderful views, but Lumo is in no frame of mind to enjoy the views when she is about to become lunch for an eagle. The eagle is probably heading back to her nest. Lumo can see the humans' wall and big lake of water behind it, far below. The wall has cut the river in two.

Out of nowhere, another huge eagle appears, with claws outstretched. Probably wants the otter. The eagle holding Lumo has no choice: she has to defend herself with her claws, and in the process, has to release Lumo from her claws. Lumo drops through the air for some distance—

SPLOOSH!!

she plunges into the big lake behind the wall—

She lands up right next to a huge golden fish. The largest fish Lumo has ever seen. With a big open mouth and big teeth. They both get a fright. Neither expecting to see the other. The first time Lumo has seen this giant fish. She wasn't expecting that!

"Good morning," says the giant fish in a deep voice. "I am a Golden Mahseer. See the golden light on my scales? That is why. And you are?"

"Smooth-coated Otter, because of the short hair."

"It's okay," says the Golden Mahseer seeing the look of fright in Lumo's eyes. "I eat fish, but I don't eat otters. Not on the menu. Relax."

A Snow Trout swims over: "You're unexpected, aren't you? Your kind is usually close to the river banks, so how did you end up in the middle of the river, out of your depth? How did you get here?"

Where to begin? wonders Lumo. How she got wings to fly over the wall and into the lake. She tries her best to tell the story.

"Well, now that you are here, can you explain this wall to us? Where did this nuisance come from?"

Other large fish crowd in: a Chocolate Mahseer, even a Goonch. Lumo tries to give them an overview—a kind of aerial picture of the wall. They have sad fish faces, all of them. Such incredibly bad news. The wall goes all the way across the river. No way around that.

"Fish do not have wings, and we do not trust eagles!" says the Golden Mahseer. "Of course, you breathe air and you can walk. As an Otter, you have paws and can go on land to get around the wall, but we fish can only swim, so we are stuck behind this wall. But we are fighting fish. We can go where you cannot go—up the river, past the big rapids." After a long fish conference, they all decide to swim upstream, take a fork to another branch of river, then downstream again to by-pass the human wall. They say goodbye to Lumo.

Lumo swims to shore, and starts going overland to get past the wall, through the forest. Keeping one eye on the sky above to avoid another eagle attack. She hasn't eaten in over a day, and she still has no idea where food will come from. Fortune smiles on her. She meets a creature that is oddly like an otter, but not one. This creature has large front teeth.

"You look like an otter but you are not!"

"Right! I am a beaver. And you look like a mess! What happened to your hair? Tell me what happened to you."

The beaver listens carefully. "You are lucky to be alive after all that," he says. "That wall is called a dam. You're an otter, I'm a beaver. The difference is that beavers build dams, but not like that. That huge dam will destroy the river, and the fish will not be able to travel up and down the river, meaning you have a big fishing problem."

"Why are they building the wall across the river?"

"The humans want the power of the river. Through the dam they can capture the power."

The beaver has been out collecting wood in the forest, chewing the wood with large front teeth, gathering it for his den, or his dam. He invites Lumo to come and see it. It is a big den, in deep water that keeps away attackers like wolves. Lumo is very hungry, with no food for over a day now. She asks the beaver for some fish. The beaver looks puzzled.

"I do not eat fish. I'm all veg—I only eat the bark of trees, and grasses and water plants." Lumo's face drops. That was not the answer she was expecting. Lumo must now look for her family, hoping they have survived. She goes back into the forest.

Lumo sends out constant otter calls—short loud chirps. And then, a few hours later, some chirps come back! Further along the river, she runs into her brother Nanda. Then Dad. They stare at each other and laugh and cry—all at the same time. This is so unexpected. All crying rivers of tears, and hugging with webbed paws. They give Lumo some fish. She eats it quickly, and they feed her some more. So hungry!

"We thought we would never see you again," says Nanda. "But where is mother?"

"At the beach. I know where. I have a kind of map in my mind."

"How is that? I mean how did you get separated?"

"Well," says Lumo, "I had an unexpected flight up the river."

She goes on to recount the story of the eagle, and tells Dad and Nanda to follow her. Lumo leads them to the beach. They spot mother in the distance. "Let me go by myself first," says Lumo. "She may not be expecting me."

Mother is standing up, trying to gather some sticks that she can use to make a new nest. Lumo sneaks up on her.

"Can I help you with that, Mum?"

Her heart skips a beat. Wait, several beats! She whirls around:

"Lumo! My little Lumo! But I thought you were…"

"Dead?"

"You're a ghost!"

"No, just plain little Lumo."

"You almost gave me a heart attack! Don't ever do that again!"

"Do what?"

"Sneak up on me like that, so unexpected!"

More heart attacks—Nanda and Dad show their faces. Tears of joy. But hugging is difficult. Mother's paws are still injured. "My paws are better, but still not good enough for fishing. These strangers are my lifeline—" she nods to another otter family. "They have been feeding me. And now you'd better tell me everything that happened, my little Lumo."

Lumo sighs. She has already told this story so many times, and she is tired. "It's a long story, Mum."

"So start with the nasty eagle then…"

Insight

Traditional Tibetans believe the mountains and streams are inhabited by divine beings. When they see an impressive tree or rock, they feel it is bound to be the abode of a sacred spirit. In traditional Tibet, we would not even dream of polluting a water source that was used by other people or animals. We believed we would incur the wrath of the sacred spirits dwelling in that river or mountain.

—HH Gyalwang Karmapa

a TRUE story from Bhutan

Dancing Like A Crane

Hands-on environmental education for school-kids: introducing Karma and Pema, the cranes who got left behind …

Gangtey Gompa, Central Bhutan

Bhutan is famous for its religious festivals that go back hundreds of years. But there's one that goes back only to 1998. The Gangtey Tsechu, or Crane Festival, takes place annually on November 11, staged in the courtyard of Gangtey Monastery, about 7 hours' drive east from Thimphu. The Crane Festival is a modern variation that combines traditional dance—mostly performed by monks—with new dance performed by school children.

The festival was started up by the Royal Society for the Protection of Nature in 1998 to draw attention to the endangered Black-necked Cranes, whose roosting grounds at Phobjikha were being encroached upon by farmers. The festival is dedicated to environmental education, with a narrative that cranes and humans can co-exist in harmony.

Black-necked Cranes nest in various parts of the Tibetan plateau and choose diverse winter migration locations across Asia. They may fly over a thousand kilometres to reach their winter roosting grounds. The festival celebrates the annual arrival of Black-necked Cranes near Gangtey Monastery in Phobjikha Valley, staying to roost until February, when they return to Tibet. The birds circle the monastery three times on arrival, before heading for nearby wetlands. These birds are regarded as symbols of good luck, beauty, grace and longevity—they live up to 30 years.

In Bhutan, the auspicious crane is revered by Buddhists as a 'lyab-bja'—meaning 'heavenly bird.' And flying at such high altitudes, it is indeed close to the heavens.

The cranes are celebrated in folk tales, poetry, song and dance—and painted into frescoes on monastery walls. The people of Phobjikha Valley plant their winter wheat only after the cranes arrive.

The valleys around Gangtey Gompa are heavily forested, with small-scale farming of potatoes and buckwheat in terraced fields. Close to Phobjikha Wetland Reserve is the Crane Visitor Centre—which acts as a small nature museum and as a spot to observe black-necked cranes in the valley through viewing scopes.

Staying right at the centre is Karma the crane—who will not be returning to Tibet after the annual migration to Bhutan. This young crane flew into Bhutan with his parents but was mauled by a feral dog. His wings cannot provide enough lift for flying. A mirror was put up in his aviary enclosure to peck at for company. In a way, Karma embodies the fate of Tibetan refugees—yearning to go back to Tibet, but unable to make the journey.

Years later, a miraculous turn of fate. Karma was on his own for four years until... Pema showed up. Pema, a young female crane, was injured and became unable to fly. She was taken to the crane centre. Against all odds, Karma has found a new friend—and a soulmate. They took some time getting used to each other, but now they play—chasing each other around their enclosure, flapping their wings. No need for a mirror anymore. They have become ambassadors for conservation of Black-necked Cranes.

In the distance, you can hear the wild cranes—noisier at dusk and dawn. Bird-watchers can access a blind on the opposite side of the valley to get a closer look at crane behaviour with binoculars and long lenses. Pairs of cranes interact—bowing, jumping and flapping wings in courtship rituals. During the day, as they fly off to find food in the valley—insects, fish, rodents, berries—you can see pairs flying in perfect formation.

A few days before Gangtey Crane Festival, about 50 birds have arrived. At the height of the season, by late November, that number can swell to over 300 cranes. Bhutan is a birders' paradise, with over 670 species identified.

Days before the festival, elaborate preparations are under way. At a monastery, monks are rehearsing moves for sacred masked dance. At the local Bayta School, boys and girls aged 9 to 14 dress up in crane costumes, practicing for their performance. This is hands-on environmental education, as the school-kids mimic the movements of the cranes, with somewhat comical results.

Education in Bhutan promotes great respect for the environment. Indeed, glowing pride in the environment is the basis for trekking and nature tourism—Bhutan's greatest tourist draws. Spiritual beliefs that sustain environmental protection are heavily imbued in Bhutanese culture—a mix of

traditional Bon and Tibetan Buddhism. Bon followers believe that guardian spirits reside in the mountains, the trees, the rivers and lakes. And that these spirits must not be disturbed through misconduct—or pollution. Offerings are made to spirits and deities to ensure the success of crops.

Excitement builds at Gangtey Monastery as the big day arrives. Bhutan's spectacular monasteries are marvels of medieval architecture that have preserved lost art-forms derived from Tibet. The crowd packed into the courtyard is mostly Bhutanese, dressed in their finest robes. Off to one side is a small pavilion with VIP seating for visiting dignitaries, who wear ceremonial white scarves reserved for entering temple grounds.

After initial speeches, the dance performances get under way. A stand-out are the majestic masked dancers—all monks. The hand-made masks depict real and mythical creatures. The dances re-enact myths, legends and moral tales: the mesmerizing dancers move slowly across the stone-paved courtyard, occasionally making acrobatic leaps into the air. A circle of women perform the Thrung Thrung Karmo dance—in praise of black-necked cranes—gracefully waving their arms like wings.

But they are not the stars of the show. The stars are the young students from Bayta School performing the Black-necked Crane dance. These students stand about the same height as an adult crane. They bob their 'beaked' heads, flap their 'wings' with glee, and comically mimic crane mating-dance ritual movements such as bowing and wing-spreading.

As the pace picks up, the students run across the courtyard in choreographed moves—adding their own vocals to the bugling of real Black-necked Cranes on the music track for this dance. And it is with this exuberant choreography seared into the memory that visitors leave the charming world of Gangtey Monastery behind.

The Black-necked Cranes themselves? Well, they stay around Gangtey until mid-February, before heading back to Tibet. They circle Gangtey Monastery three times before they wing their way north.

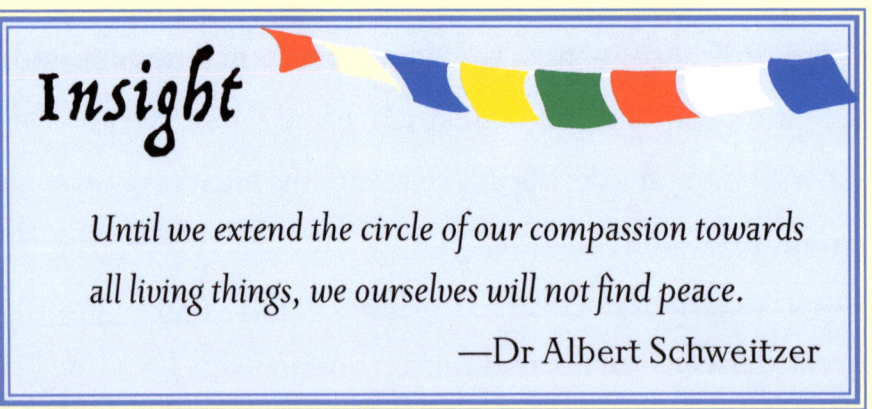

Insight

Until we extend the circle of our compassion towards all living things, we ourselves will not find peace.
—Dr Albert Schweitzer

Video Links

Black-necked Crane dance from NYTSC with crane vocal sounds in background:
vimeo.com/577108872

White Cranes of the Gods, sung by Kelsang Chukie Tethong
vimeo.com/587369349

eXtreme Animals from Tibet

Latin	Tibetan	Altitude range
Panthera uncia	*ganzig (also: saa)*	*3,000 to 6,000 metres*

Snow Leopard

The Snow Leopard is thought to require a territory of 200 square kilometres as its home. Unique in its camouflage - a greyish spotted coat, blending in with its terrain - the Snow Leopard is mostly active at dusk and dawn, and particularly fond of stalking Blue Sheep, Ibex and Himalayan Marmots. By day it sleeps in caves or on rocky ledges. It inhabits remote high-altitude terrain, and is spread across Central Asia, from Mongolia to India. The largest numbers left are in northwest India - in Ladakh, Spiti and Lahaul.

    The Snow Leopard is about the size of a large dog. It has adapted ingeniously to life in extreme snowy terrain: its large paws act like snowshoes. Its enormous tail is used to stabilise acrobatic leaps - and at night is wrapped around body and face like a scarf to withstand freezing temperatures. After mating season, the female Snow Leopard retreats to a den to give birth. The diligent mother raises her offspring alone, providing food and shelter for her cubs - for up to 2 years, while they learn essential hunting skills.

Superpowers

For hunting, this leopard relies on camouflage, stealth and a huge leap. To bring its prey down, the Snow Leopard relies on the incredible spring of its powerful hind legs, which enable it to leap high into the air and for considerable length. The leopard can jump 1.8 metres into the air with no running start, and can leap 15 metres across a ravine: it can change direction swiftly to tackle its prey. So elusive and stealthy is the Snow Leopard that the first movie film to capture it in action was not taken until the dawn of the 21st century. Due to its superb camouflage, you could be standing close to a snow leopard and still not see it.

Fun Facts

Because of its throat-bone structure, the Snow Leopard is a non-roaring cat, but is known to make strange howling cries during the January – March mating season. This odd sound is called yowling. In Bhutan, parents use yowling as proof that Yetis are around – as a way of keeping errant kids in line. The Snow Leopard may have striking blue eyes. Or grey, or green eyes. At birth, more likely to have blue eyes, which can change colour after 8 months or so. This is in contrast with other large cats that usually have yellowish eyes.

Fact or Fiction?

In the story, the park ranger makes friends with an injured Snow Leopard. Does this actually happen? No. There may be bonding between a zoo-born Snow Leopard and its handlers, but as it grows older, the leopard becomes more aloof. Snow Leopards do not even make friends with other Snow Leopards – except for immediate family. Some Snow Leopard pairs or brothers may hunt together. In the story, the Snow Leopard attacks a human. In reality, do Snow Leopards attack humans? No cases have been recorded. There have been cases where a Snow Leopard has entered a sheep pen, and when discovered by the herder, panics and bowls over the herder at the gate. Unlike other leopards, the Snow Leopard is extremely unlikely to attack a human.

Saving the Snow Leopard

The Snow Leopard is highly endangered, with numbers remaining estimated at 4,000 to 7,000 across their range. Threats include poaching for its fur, and for parts used in Traditional Chinese Medicine. Herders will kill Snow Leopards that try to take their sheep or other livestock. Insurance to pay herders for lost livestock has been introduced in places like Spiti to stop herders killing Snow Leopards. Herders pay an annual premium, then make a claim if any livestock is lost. An estimated 600 Snow Leopards are found in zoos. Can captive breeding save the Snow Leopard? Highly unlikely. Over generations, captive Snow Leopards lose knowledge about survival in nature. Released back into the wild, they would likely not survive. In captivity, they can lose the incredible spring that enables them to capture fast-moving prey. This is due to atrophy of muscles that are no longer used. For more about Snow Leopards, visit: *snowleopard.org*

Latin	Tibetan	Altitude range
Ailurus fulgens	*dhomtra marchung*	*1,500 to 4,800 metres*

Red Panda

This handsome mammal has long been thought to be a distant relative of the Giant Panda because it shares the peculiar habit of feeding largely on bamboo, and because it has similar teeth and paws. But Red Pandas are actually more closely related to raccoons. This chestnut-coloured 'cat-bear' is small, with a ringed bushy tail half its length. The Red Panda's diet consists mostly of bamboo. Unlike the Giant Panda, which eats every part of the bamboo plant (except the roots), the Red Panda only eats the youngest, most tender shoots and leaves. The Giant Panda relies totally on bamboo, but the Red Panda branches out. While the Red Panda's diet is about two-thirds bamboo, the remaining third is surprisingly diverse: on the menu are mushrooms, fruit, roots, acorns, lichens, and grasses – and they have been observed eating insects and fish.

The Red Panda ranges much higher in elevation than the Giant Panda, inhabiting terrain from 1,500 to 4,800 metres. It is nocturnal and spends most of its life in the trees, living in mountainous deciduous and conifer forests, and dense bamboo forests of the Tibetan plateau, including western Sichuan and Yunnan, Nepal, northeastern India, Bhutan, and northern Burma. A sub-species *Ailurus fulgens styani* is found only in Sichuan and Yunnan (China) and northern Burma.

Superpowers

Weird but true, the Red Panda can rotate its ankles 180 degrees when climbing down a tree, enabling it to go down head-first. Only a few animals on the planet can do this. Raccoons share this skill – they can come down trees nose first. The Red Panda also has an 'extra thumb' – an enlarged wrist-bone that helps when grabbing tree branches and bamboo stems. It is actually a semi-opposable thumb. And for extra grip, the Red Panda will also use its long tail to hook onto branches. Well-adapted to cold winters, the Red Panda uses its long bushy tail as a blanket when needed.

Fun Facts

When cornered or threatened, the Red Panda will stand up on its hind legs to make itself appear larger, and will extend its front paws upwards for the same reason – ready to slash out with sharp claws. It might also vocalize with a loud grumbly bark noise. Red Pandas use a variety of sounds to communicate, including squeals, twitters and huff-quacks. A huff-quack is a sound halfway between that made by a pig and a duck. To signal danger, Red Pandas hiss or grunt. The charismatic Red Panda appears as the character Master Shifu in the Kung Fu Panda films. A rolled-up Red Panda is the logo for the internet browser Firefox.

Fact or fiction?

Does the Red Panda eat chillies, as in the story?

No, chilli peppers are not part of the Red Panda's diet. But there is another mammal living in the trees of Yunnan that loves eating hot peppers: the Tree Shrew. Apart from humans, the long-nosed Tree Shrew is the only known mammal that is reckless enough to consume chilli peppers – and actually enjoy them (birds have no problem consuming peppers).

Saving the Red Panda

This mammal is highly endangered. Fewer than 10,000 remain in the wild. Threats to survival are mainly loss of habitat due to deforestation at the edge of the Tibetan plateau, to make furniture and chopsticks. Red Pandas are poached in India and trafficked to China for the pet trade and private resorts. In the Chinese province of Yunnan, the Red Panda is hunted for its pelt, used to make traditional hats. For more information about Red Pandas, visit: *redpandanetwork.org*

Latin	Tibetan	Altitude range
Gyps himalayensis	*jagoe*	*from lowlands up to 7,000 metres*

Himalayan Griffon Vulture

Actually, some Himalayan Griffon vultures have been sighted riding 'blue thermals' near the summit of Everest, at altitudes of over 8,000 metres. Himalayan Griffons are huge birds – perhaps the largest and heaviest in the region. They have a large wingspan – extending 2.5 metres to 3 metres in adults. As with other vultures, the bird feeds mainly from carcasses of animals. With one peculiar twist in Tibet: this bird gathers in clusters at sky burial ceremonies to consume human corpses. It is thus an iconic bird in Tibetan lore. In Tibetan, *jhator* (sky burial) means 'offering to the birds'. The Bearded Vulture (Lammergeier) also shows up at sky burial ceremonies.

This vulture bides its time because it largely feeds on bones. How can a bird eat bones? The Bearded Vulture flies off with a bone to great height, drops it, and then swoops to feed on the marrow inside the cracked bone. The Parsees of India also follow this custom of sky burial. They may not be the prettiest of bird species, but Himalayan Griffons perform important duties as scavengers, clearing dead animals that cause disease if left to rot. This is sociable eating, as a kettle of vultures descends on a dead animal.

Superpowers

Griffon vultures have incredible eyesight. They can spot a carcass from a distance of 3 kilometres. Himalayan Griffons are Old World Vultures, primarily relying on sharp eyesight to locate food. Their featherless heads make them different from New World Vultures, which locate prey with a keen sense of smell. In fact New World Vultures have a sense of smell that is the best among bird species. Why? To determine how old the dead meat is. If not "fresh," the meat could be dangerous to consume.

Saving the Himalayan Griffon

Himalayan Griffons are in big trouble as a species. The major threat to their survival is poison. Across the Indian sub-continent, vulture populations have dropped, in some areas plummeting over 90 percent since the 1990s. This is from eating dead livestock laced with the drug Diclofenac, an anti-inflammatory used by farmers to treat cows and buffaloes. Diclofenac causes fatal kidney damage in birds that eat carcasses. Solution: there is another drug called Meloxicam, which farmers could use, but it is more expensive. The use of Meloxicam would not kill vultures. Himalayan Griffon Vultures have fared much better than other vulture species and have not suffered the same precipitous decline. One source of food for Griffons in Tibet is dwindling: there are fewer yak carcasses to eat due to mass settlement of Tibetan nomads by Chinese authorities and slaughtering of their yaks and livestock.

Bar-Headed Goose

Latin	Tibetan	Altitude range
Anser indicus	*ngangpa*	*lowlands up to 6,500 metres*

This goose takes its name from two black bars visible behind its eyes. Astronauts on the wing: Bar-headed Geese can fly at very high altitude, clearing the Himalaya twice each year to complete an epic migration. They have been observed flying over mountain passes at 5,500 metres, and even on occasion as high as 6,500 metres, even 7,000 metres. For many years, it was believed that no birds flew over the high peaks of the Himalaya. Now, it appears that half a dozen species do fly over the world's highest peaks, the ultimate high-fliers of the avian world. Yellow-billed Choughs have been sighted at altitudes of 7,000 metres by climbers attempting Everest, and Snow Pigeons have been spotted flying over peaks at 8,300 metres. When winter is over, Bar-headed Geese leave their feeding-grounds in the lowlands of Nepal and India, going from near sea level straight up to 6,000 or 7,000 metres, heading past mighty Himalayan peaks to breeding grounds in Amdo (Kokonor, aka Qinghai Lake), Outer Mongolia and Kyrgyzstan.

Bar-headed Geese have been clocked flying at 80 km/hr, but with a tailwind they can rocket along at up to 160 km/hr. How does the Bar-headed Goose manage to fly at such extreme altitude? An inner layer of down feathers helps stop the bird from freezing to death, while an outer layer of tightly woven feathers apparently waterproofs the goose and prevents build-up of body ice that would cause the bird to plunge to its doom. The honking of the Bar-headed Goose in the mountains is a sure sign you are in Tibet.

Latin	Tibetan	Altitude range
Pantholops hodgsonii	*chiru* (also: *tso*)	3,500 to 5,500 metres

Tibetan Antelope

The Tibetan Antelope inhabits high desert plateau. The females are hornless, but the males sport a pair of long slender upright horns, which could make them the source of unicorn myths in Tibet that date back several centuries (viewed in profile, the chiru would appear to have just one long horn). A male uses his lyre-shaped horns to spar with rivals when protecting his harem. The males have black markings on legs and face that the females do not have. The Latin name for the antelope is derived from Brian Houghton Hodgson, who first described the animal for Western science in 1834. This antelope is only found on the Tibetan plateau.

The chiru's underwool, known as *shahtoosh*, is the finest animal fibre in the world. The chiru has never been tamed or reared in captivity: the only way to get *shahtoosh* is through killing the animals and skinning them. Although the trade in *shahtoosh* is now illegal, it has pushed the chiru to the brink of extinction, with an estimated 200,000 or so remaining in the wild. Another solution is to focus on *pashmina* – which is high-grade wool from cashmere goats – as a commercial product. Chiru cannot be kept in captivity and raised for their underwool – they will not survive in captivity.

Superpowers

The chiru's fine wool is a special adaptation that traps layers of warm air close to its body so it can survive snow blizzards where the thermometer plummets to minus 40°C. The chiru can outrun predators on the plateau – sprinting at up to 80 km per hour. But it cannot outrun hunters in jeeps with high-powered weapons.

Fact or fiction?

In the story, Khandro the crow accepts a gift of antelope underwool to line her nest and make it soft and cosy for eggs. Is that true in reality? Well, yes and no. Red-billed Choughs line their twig nest with hair and wool. Not clear where the wool comes from, but the hair is likely to be from the Himalayan Tahr – 'harvested' from a live Tahr.

Saving the Tibetan Antelope

The Tibetan Antelope is highly endangered. The main threat to survival is poaching of antelopes to get their underwool, used to make fine scarves and shawls for wealthy buyers. Each shawl made of antelope underwool is equivalent to three to five dead antelopes. The Tibetan Antelope is fully protected in Tibet, and the trade in Tibetan Antelope underwool has been banned in India, where Kashmir is the main location for shawl-making, but poaching still goes on. Tibetan Antelope horns are ground up and used for traditional medicine purposes, supposedly for 'fever' and 'lung diseases.' There is absolutely no proof that this works.

Latin	Tibetan	Altitude range
Ursus arctos pruinosus	dremong	lowlands up to 5,000 metres

Tibetan Brown Bear

While its hair is black, the Tibetan Brown Bear's outer hair shows a blue-grey sheen, which is why this species is also known as the Tibetan Blue Bear. Like most bears, the Tibetan Brown Bear can stand on its hind legs to get a better view of its surroundings, or sniff the place out. This highly endangered bear is normally found in forests, but also ranges into open high-altitude zones in Qinghai and Tibet. Closely related is the Himalayan Brown Bear, *Ursus arctos isabellinus*, from the central and western Himalayan regions.

Tibetan Brown Bears eat anything they can find: grasses, roots, bulbs and other plants, insects and small mammals such as marmots, pikas and voles. In the autumn they descend to lower levels to feast on fruit and berries. They will also take sheep and goats and feed upon carrion when found.

Tibetan Brown Bears are mostly solitary, except during the May-June mating season. Cubs are born in the winter den in December and January. The bears go into hibernation in a cave or dug-out den around October, emerging in April or May. They can sleep for up to six months without drinking water or eating food. The arrival of warmer weather causes the bear to awake from this deep sleep, but this is becoming earlier each year because of global heating.

Confusing Bears

Lower down in altitude is the smaller Asiatic Black Bear (*Ursus thibetanus laniger*), found in mountainous forests of Yunnan, Sichuan and other parts. This species has a distinctive white or creamy crescent-shaped patch on its chest. It is also known as the 'Moon Bear' because of this patch. With similar markings is the Sun Bear, found in Yunnan and in parts of Southeast Asia. Another resident of low-altitude forest in Nepal and Bhutan is the Sloth Bear, which can be extremely aggressive toward humans. Bears of the Himalayan region are little understood, and there are possibly more species and subspecies than those mentioned.

Fact or fiction?

Is there a connection between the Tibetan Brown Bear and the Yeti? Yes, unlike other Asian bears, the Tibetan Brown Bear stands tall: females can stand up to 1.8 metres, and males can stand up to 2.2 metres tall – as tall as a basketball player. Which is probably why the species (and its huge footprint) are likely to be mistaken for a Yeti. All current research via DNA analysis traces the Yeti back to the Tibetan Brown Bear, *Ursus arctos pruinos*, or its cousin *Ursus arctos isabellinus*. And that's the un-bear-able truth about the Yeti.

The postage stamp at right is of an archer taking on a Yeti in Bhutan. Bhutan hosts the world's only nature reserve devoted to allowing the Yeti to roam around free. This is Sakteng Nature Reserve, to the far east of Bhutan.

THE ABOMINABLE SNOWMAN

Saving the Tibetan Brown Bear

This species is at risk from trophy hunting, and from poaching for Traditional Chinese Medicine. The main species sought for TCM are the Asiatic Black Bear and the Sun Bear. Various body parts are used in TCM 'cures', such as bear-paw soup. The main part sought for TCM is bile from live bears held in tiny cages on bear farms. Thousands of bears are held captive in bear-bile farms in China and Vietnam. Bears produce more bile than any other mammal. Bear-bile is used to treat liver and other ailments in humans, but there is little proof that it works as medicine. In any case, the active ingredient, known as ursodiol, can be synthesised in a lab, so no need to get it from live bears.

Latin	Tibetan	Altitude range
Budorcas taxicolor	bamen (also: *ragya*)	*1,000 to 4,500 metres*

Takin

The Takin is a hairy hoofed herbivore with a bulbous nose and backward-facing horns. It is a strange mix of moose, musk-ox, wildebeest, goat and antelope, and can weigh up to 400 kilograms, with a body up to two metres long. Both males and females have horns. The male is larger and has a distinct black dorsal stripe along his spine. The Takin favours the eastern Tibetan plateau, particularly in southeast Tibet and in Bhutan, where it inhabits dense forest. It moves to alpine zones in the spring to avoid leeches and bugs. The naturalist who first identified the Takin for Western science in 1850 never saw a live one. Brian Houghton Hodgson, the British Resident in Kathmandu, Nepal, dispatched native assistants to find rare animals. They would bring back skins and describe the animal's behaviour. With no way to observe the animal himself, Hodgson was uncertain where to place the Takin on the tree of life. His confusion is reflected in the scientific name he gave the species: *Budorcas taxicolor*, meaning 'oxlike gazelle, badger- coloured'. The puzzle continues to this day.

    In Bhutan, studies show that the Takin's diet is highly versatile, with different plant species consumed in summer and winter due to varying elevations traversed. Research has identified more than 65 plant species that the Takin feeds on. It can rear up on its hind legs to munch on low-lying branches of birch and willow trees. About 66 per cent of its summer diet consists of shrubs; grasses make up around 14 percent, and the rest is from herbs and low-lying trees. In connection with mating rituals, Takin bulls vocalise with a cross between a muffled roar and an elaborate belch. Another male vocalisation is a loud coughing sound – to raise the alarm if the herd is threatened by predators.

Takin subspecies

There are four subspecies: Mishmi Takin (Tibet), Shensi Takin and Sichuan Takin (China), and the Bhutan Takin. The one shown at right is a male Bhutan Takin, with photo taken in captivity as this is one of a handful of Takins kept in a reserve overlooking Thimphu. The Bhutan Takin is the national animal of Bhutan and there are heavy penalties for poaching.

Superpowers

Though large, the Takin is very sure-footed on difficult, slippery terrain due to the firm grip of its hooves. It is an agile climber on steep rock.

Fact or fiction?

The Takin is the stuff of myth. For starters, many descriptions suggest that the Takin's shaggy yellow coat could be the fabled Golden Fleece sought by Jason and the Argonauts in ancient Greek legend, although in economic terms, the Golden Fleece might more easily be applied to the underwool of the Tibetan Antelope. In Bhutan, the Takin is revered, its origin attributed to the folk hero Drukpa Kunley. In the 16th century, this crazy Tantric master was asked by followers to perform a miracle at the end of a feast. Drukpa Kunley took a heap of cow and goat bones and reassembled them into a new animal – essentially grafting the head of a goat onto the body of a cow.

Do Takins make their own trails? Yes, in fact some explorers have used Takin trails to access remote places like Hidden Falls on the Yarlung Tsangpo. Are there tigers at altitude in Bhutan? Yes, Bengal tiger tracks have been found at 4,000 metres in Bhutan. They are moving higher due to climate change factors.

Saving the Takin

Probably fewer than 5,000 Takins remain in the wild. They are killed for meat and hides, and in trophy hunting. The best bet for survival of the species is excellent protection in Bhutan.

Wild Yak bull in the Changtang
Photo by Dan Miller

Latin	Tibetan	Altitude range
Bos mutus	*drong*	*3,000 to 5,600 metres*

Wild Yak

In Tibetan, the word 'yak' refers to the male of the species, while the female is called 'dri' or 'nak.' In English and other languages that borrow the word, 'yak' is commonly used for both sexes. The Wild Yak is an enormous creature: an adult male can weigh up to a tonne (double the weight of a domestic yak), and can stand almost two metres high at the shoulder. In fact, the wild yak is the third largest mammal in Asia, after the Asian elephant and the rhino. *Bos mutus* is the Latin name given to distinguish the Wild Yak from the domestic one. The domestic yak is designated *Bos grunniens*, which means 'grunting ox' – a nod to the yak's habit of grunting when agitated or when calling their young. Wild Yaks grunt during mating season. Domestic pack-yaks can carry loads up to 6,400m at Everest ABC.

    Wild Yaks graze mostly on grasses, mosses and herbs. There are around 60 kinds of grass on the menu. Wild Yaks are grasslands friendly as they nibble grass, and do not pull grass out at the roots (as domestic cashmere goats do). Like antelopes, goats and other grass-eaters, wild yaks have no upper front teeth – just hard gums. But they have upper back teeth. In winter, yaks use their horns and hooves to break through snow to forage for plants beneath. Yaks are superbly adapted to altitude: so much so that they cannot survive at lower elevations. Wild yaks may assemble in small herds of females, calves and a few bulls. Or they could be small bachelor groups of older males. They are nimble and sure-footed over rough terrain. Herds travel on snow in single file, carefully stepping in footprints left by the lead yak.

Superpowers

The Wild Yak's long shaggy coat enables it to withstand violent winds and snowstorms. Under its fur, the yak secrete a sticky sweat that tangles to form a thick protective blanket. The Wild Yak is able to survive freezing temperatures in harsh winters, when it can dip to minus 40 degrees Celsius. In fact, Wild Yaks have been observed swimming in nearly frozen water.

Fact or fiction?

In the story, there is mixing of Wild Yaks and domestic yaks. Does this happen? Yes, Wild Yaks will interact with domestic yaks, especially in the July to September mating season. And that's a huge problem for nomad herders as the resulting new-born yaks are unruly and difficult to deal with. Do yaks sing? Well, no. But rather like pro tennis players, they grunt a lot. However, there is a dog species that does sing. This is the Singing Dog, thought to be extinct but found again in Papua New Guinea. Singing Dogs make yodelling sounds: when one dog starts up, others will join in with different vocals, somewhat like an orchestra.

Saving the Wild Yak

The Wild Yak is considered extinct in Nepal and Bhutan. In early 20th century Tibet, travellers witnessed huge herds of Wild Yaks and Kyang (Tibetan wild asses) on the grasslands, along with other grazers like antelopes and gazelles. They could hear the herds too, with the thundering hooves of Wild Yak herds. This is all gone. Hunting by Chinese military and settlers has reduced the millions of Wild Yaks to fewer than 10,000 remaining. A sighting of Wild Yaks is rare today, though possible in very remote parts of the Changthang or in Amdo, northeast Tibet. A Wild Yak may be sighted as a solitary individual or in small groups.

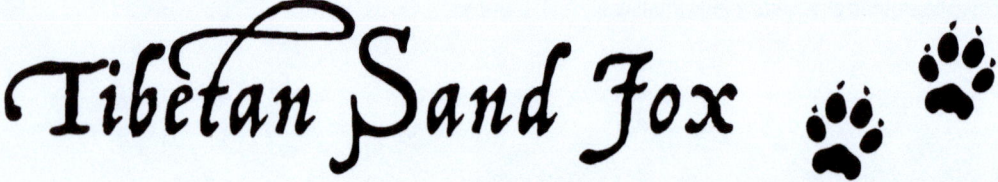

Photo by Tshering Tobgay

Latin	Tibetan	Altitude range
Vulpes ferrilata	*waser*	3,000 to 5,300 metres

Tibetan Sand Fox

The first thing you notice about this animal is the bizarre shape of its head. The head is large and squarish, unlike any other fox. The Tibetan Sand Fox is only found on the Tibetan plateau. This fox mates for life and lives in a den, raising two to four pups. Partners may hunt together. The main diet is pikas, also known as rock-rabbits. The sneaky Tibetan Sand Fox has been known to follow the Tibetan Brown Bear, hoping to catch pikas as they flee from the bear, which digs up their burrows. Sand Foxes also eat rodents, woolly hares, marmots, rabbits, lizards and small birds. And plants, such as berries.

    The Sand Fox's large head, chubby cheeks and stubby limbs give it an almost cartoonish appearance. Although first described in 1842 by Brian Houghton Hodgson, the British Resident in Kathmandu, he never saw a live one. This fox is so stealthy that even today sighting one is a supreme challenge: the Sand Fox was captured on film in 2006, for the BBC series *Planet Earth*, Episode 7. The Himalayan Red Fox (*Vulpes vulpes*) inhabits similar terrain, and despite its name ranges in colour from reddish to brown or even greyish. There are at least 8 subspecies of this Red Fox.

Superpowers

The Sand Fox's yellowish-grey coat makes it a master of disguise in rocky and semi- desert terrain. Pretending to be a rock is not easy to do. The squarish head enables it to look more rock-like. Like all foxes, the Sand Fox has a keen sense of hearing and smell, enabling it to catch its main prey, the Pika. Little is known about the Sand Fox, but its sense of smell is likely to be many thousands of times more sensitive than that of humans.

Fact or fiction?

In the story, pikas are moving to higher ground because they love the cold and cannot take the heat. Is this true? Yes, it is happening – and eventually the pikas might run out of grass to eat at higher altitude.

In the story, a Black Fox appears. Is there such a creature in Tibet? Actually, this is a Red Fox, covered in coal dust. The idea is taken from black chickens and other blackened animals that appeared in the city of Wuhai after large-scale coal-mining started there. Over 400 factories have sprouted up in this city in Inner Mongolia. The Tibetan Sand Fox shares much of its range with the similar-sized Red Fox, but there is little competition between the two species as the Red Fox hunts at night, and the Sand Fox hunts by day.

Saving the Tibetan Sand Fox

The best known predator of the Sand Fox is humans. The Sand Fox is hunted for its luxurious pelt. Humans are killing the Sand Fox in other ways: a Chinese grasslands program to poison pikas has been on-going for more than 40 years. There is no proof that poisoning pikas is a sound grasslands management strategy. In fact, pikas, by digging tunnels, make the grasslands more accessible to birds for nesting. The Tibetan Sand Fox should be protected in national parks in Tibet, but the question is whether these are genuine or not. They are more likely to be Paper Parks – existing on paper only. That includes Hoh Xil World Heritage Site and Changtang National Nature Reserve (which covers 334,000 square km – the second largest park in the world).

Photo by Tshering Tobgay

Latin	Tibetan
Lutrogale perspicillata	*surm*
Altitude range	
prefers lower elevations of 1,000 metres or less, but has been tracked up to 3,600 metres	

Smooth-coated Otter

Smooth-coated Otters are found in freshwater regions in Bhutan, Nepal, India, Bangladesh, SW Yunnan, and much further afield in Sumatra. Their diet is 70 percent fish, typically fish from 5 to 30 cm long. They also hunt on land, eating reptiles, frogs, insects, crustaceans and small mammals. When fishing, they may hunt in groups, sometimes with up to ten Smooth-coated Otters swimming upstream in a V formation.

They spend the night in dens, dug under tree roots, or in dense vegetation, or among boulders. Some build a more permanent structure, similar to that of a beaver dam, with an underwater entrance and a tunnel that leads to a nest above water. The female otter guards a litter of up to 6 pups. Smooth-coated otters communicate with vocalisations such as whistles, chirps and wails, and use scent glands to mark territory. There are several otter species in Asia: the Smooth-coated Otter, the Asian Small-clawed Otter (often found in irrigated rice fields), and the Eurasian Otter. The Smooth-coated Otter is the largest otter species found in Asia.

Superpowers

The Smooth-coated Otter has webbed paws that allow for great manual dexterity in grabbing things – like fish. When swimming fast, the Smooth-coated Otter tucks in its shorter front paws and uses its webbed hind feet and tail for propulsion. It can close its ears and nostrils when diving underwater. These otters have been known to create and use tools, similar to monkeys. A favourite tool for otters is a small smooth rock, used to open mollusks and clams. The otters like to 'juggle' rocks – swiftly passing one or more stones around between the chest, hands and mouth. Nobody knows why otters engage in juggling rocks. Perhaps just for fun.

Fun Facts

Smooth-coated Otters have been photographed engaging in human-like behaviour, like holding hands. Otters love to sunbathe during the day: they hunt at night. Although a good swimmer and fish-catcher, the otter cannot hold its breath underwater for long.

Saving the Smooth-coated Otter

Making life very difficult for otters are human intrusions on their habitat, like building of roads, and destruction of wetlands for agriculture. The biggest threat is hydroelectric dams. Otters are affected by water pollution due to run-off of pesticides and fertilizers for agriculture. Poaching occurs in Nepal, India and Bangladesh – the otter fur is highly prized. There is some evidence that young otter pups are sold in the pet trade in Asia. The Karnali River is one of the last free-flowing rivers sourced in Tibet. There are plans for large dams to be built by both Chinese and Indian engineers. All the major rivers sourced in Tibet are being heavily dammed by Chinese engineers, and this blocks fish migration, spawning and breeding patterns.

Latin	Tibetan	Altitude range
Grus nigricollis	*trung trung*	*from lowlands up to 4,500 m.*

Black-necked Crane

The Black-necked Cranes of Tibet were the last of the 15 crane species to be described, after they were found near Lake Kokonor on the remote Tibetan plateau in 1876 by Russian naturalist Nikolai Przhevalsky. The only alpine crane species, this is the tallest of the birds in Tibet, up to 1.5m high. Much of its height is in the neck, which is black with a red cap. There may be fewer than 12,000 Black-necked Cranes remaining in the wild. This Tibetan crane breeds at high-altitude lakes, wetlands and riverine marshes in central and eastern Tibet, and migrates to spend the winter (November through March) in Bhutan, northeast India and western China.

They eat roots, tubers, invertebrates (including insects and shrimp), small vertebrates (such as lizards and frogs), and grain. In Tibet, nesting on grassy islands or building in the water, they construct their nests by lining scrapes with reeds, or making piles of mud, grass, rushes and other plants. Both parents incubate the eggs – never leaving the nest unattended unless threatened. The chicks have black-and-gray body plumage, and cinnamon-brown head. They take two or three years to reach adulthood, live an average of 14 years, and can live as long as 30 years.

Heavenly Bird

In a mating ritual dance, both the female and male bow to each other with wings wide-open, leap into the air in synchronized rhythm, and make loud clicking and bugling sounds. Elaborate courtship displays and dances are followed by collaborative nest building – and mating. In Buddhist lore, Black-necked Cranes are regarded as highly auspicious, and are painted in temple frescoes. Black-necked Cranes closely resemble Red-crowned Cranes (*Grus japonensis*), a crane species that is highly revered in Japan, and also found in NE China, Mongolia and Siberia.

Saving the Black-necked Crane

This bird is threatened by habitat loss and degradation, pollution, environmental contamination, illegal hunting, collection of their eggs, human disturbance, and predation from stray dogs. Find out more at the International Crane Foundation website: *savingcranes.org*

This covers all 15 crane species, with lots of details.

Wheel of Crane Conservation

Author taking part in presentation on Tibet environment issues at Gopalpur Tibetan Children's Village (TCV) near Dharamsala. Speaking about Tibetan animals, asking lots of questions…

SOME QUESTIONS

KARLHA the very curious Himalayan Griffon asks many many questions—often not getting clear answers. But you should be able to find answers to the following questions from details found in this book.

If you should meet a Snow Leopard, what should you do? Run? Can a human make friends with a Snow Leopard?

Can captive breeding save a species like the Snow Leopard? Will captive-bred animals survive if released into the wild?

The Himalayan Griffon lives on a non-veg diet. But a very special non-veg diet. What kind?

What happens when a Himalayan Griffon vulture eats too much?

What is the legend from Bhutan about how the Takin was created?

Why do yaks grunt? What are two special words for female yaks?

The Wild Yak is the third-largest animal in Asia. What are the first and second largest animals in Asia?

Why do Takins fight over salt?

How long does the Tibetan Brown Bear sleep in winter?

What is the biggest honey bee in the world?

Why does the Tibetan Sand Fox have a square-ish head?
Does this fox have a good sense of smell?
What is the Smooth-coated Otter's favourite tool? Why?

How long can the Black-necked Crane live? Why are these cranes known as 'Heavenly Birds'?

Which Tibetan animal has the finest wool in the world?

Which animal is the Red Panda most closely related to?

Which Tibetan animal makes an odd sound at night which some say is the mythical Yeti?

Comparisons
Which Tibetan animal in this book is the most dangerous?

Which animal is the biggest by weight?

Which animal can run the fastest?

Which animal in this book goes to the highest altitude?

What is the most important creature in this book?

What superpower do you admire most in the Tibetan animals shown in this book?

A.M.A. WITH THE RED PANDA

📷 @bam_boo

Ask me anything!

Type here...

THREE THINGS YOU JUST CANNOT DO WITHOUT?

BAMBOO, BAMBOO & BAMBOO.

ISN'T IT LONELY BEING THE ONLY MEMBER IN THE FAMILY 'AILURIDAE'?

I'M A SOLITARY ANIMAL, SO IT WORKS FOR ME!

YOUR TOP BINGE-WATCH RECOMMENDATION?
WATCHING BAMBOO STEMS SWAY IN THE BREEZE. IT'S NOT JUST ENTERTAINMENT; IT'S THERAPY!

FAVOURITE CARTOON CHARACTER - KICHI, OR MASTER SHIFU?

MASTER SHIFU'S GOT THAT RED PANDA ATTITUDE; SO HIM.

FAVOURITE DRINK?

RICE BEER IN A BAMBOO BARREL. THOSE AROMAS MIXING — OH MY GOD!

CHROME OR FIREFOX?

PLEASE ASK BETTER QUESTIONS.

HOW ARE YOU RELATED TO THE GIANT PANDA?

HE'S A DISTANT RELATIVE WHO I BUMP INTO AT WEDDINGS. I'M ACTUALLY MORE CLOSELY RELATED TO WEASELS.

THEN WHY THE NAME PANDA?

IT WAS SUPPOSED TO BE 'POONYA' ('BAMBOO EATER' IN A NEPALI DIALECT). BUT, EUROPEANS, I TELL YOU!

FAVOURITE FILM?

GUNJAN MENON'S 'THE FIREFOX GUARDIAN'. P.S.- I'M IN IT!

YOUR IDEA OF A PERFECT DATE?

GNAWING ON THE SAME BAMBOO SHOOT FROM OPPOSITE ENDS, ENDING IN A KISS.

YOUR MOST TRUSTED COMPANION?

MY BUSHY TAIL.

WHAT DOES THE COLOUR RED MEAN TO YOU?

AS OF NOW, MY IUCN STATUS: ENDANGERED!

The Himalayan Brown Bear is widely believed to have inspired the legend of the Yeti.

MOUNTAINEERING TIPS FROM HIMALAYAN ANIMALS

INVEST IN FOOLPROOF INSULATION.

—The Pallas' Cat

TAKE YOUR STAMINA-BUILDING REGIME SERIOUSLY.

—The Kiang

GET THE RIGHT FOOTWEAR FOR A STURDY GRIP.

—The Himalayan Tahr

STOCK UP ON FOOD SUPPLIES.

—The Himalayan Marmot

LISTEN TO THE MOUNTAINS MORE THAN YOU SPEAK.

—The Tibetan Lynx

YOU CANNOT FLY HIGH WITHOUT EXERCISING YOUR PECTORALS.

—The Black-necked Crane

NEVER DISCOUNT THE IMPORTANCE OF TEAMWORK IN CONQUERING A SUMMIT.

—The Brahminy Shelduck

A TRUE MOUNTAINEER IS HIS OWN PORTER.

—The Snow Leopard

AND A TRUE MOUNTAINEER NEVER LEAVES BEHIND ANY LITTER.

—The Bearded Vulture

The Real Antelope Detective

For reasons that are unclear, in the 1980s there was a sudden surge of interest in *shahtoosh* shawls and scarves in fashion boutiques in the West, sold to socialites and movie stars for up to US$5,000 apiece. Larger shawls could sell for up to US$20,000 each. The *shahtoosh* shawls and scarves quickly became status symbols.

In 1991, American wildlife expert Dr George Schaller received a letter from Michael Sautman, a Californian who was running cashmere processing plants in Mongolia and Tibet. Sautman had received a request from a firm in Italy for 500 kilograms of *shahtoosh*. Intrigued, Sautman and Schaller delved deeper. They knew the wool came from the Changtang region. Traders said it was the underwool of the Ibex, but Schaller knew there were few ibex in the Changtang. However, Schaller had seen a lot of antelope carcasses at a nomad camp in the Changtang, and Sautman had seen *shahtoosh* arriving in Lhasa for shipment to Kashmir.

Comparing notes, the two men came to the conclusion that *shahtoosh* is the underwool of the Tibetan Antelope. Drop-dead gorgeous: the antelope was being shot in large numbers in Tibet to feed a fashion craze in Hong Kong, Milan, Paris, London and New York. Recent research has revealed that *shahtoosh* is the finest animal fibre in the world—finer than the hair of the Vicuna (South America) or the Arctic Musk-ox. The Tibetan Antelope's wool is a special adaptation that traps layers of warm air close to its body so it can tolerate freezing temperatures—the key to its survival in the extreme environment of Tibet.

To get this wool, Tibetan and Chinese hunters have to shoot the antelope. The chiru cannot be tamed or reared in captivity—and in any case, it would probably die from the cold if its underwool were shorn (and conversely, it might not grow the wool at all if conditions are not cold or windy enough). Then Sautman and Schaller realised there was another identification problem: after the antelopes were shot and the underwool shorn off, this would be mixed in with fine cashmere wool for contraband transport. It was only with the advent of a specific DNA test that the raw wool could be identified as *shahtoosh*—or that a shawl could be determined to be made from *shahtoosh* rather than cashmere or pashmina. Of course, experts can determine this by hand, but DNA testing provided proof.

George Schaller found that the Tibetan Antelope was already fully protected under Indian law. He mounted a successful campaign to have the *shahtoosh* trade banned in Kashmir in 2000, and shipments of shawls were seized around the world. With demand down, the killing of antelopes tapered off in the early 2000s. However, poaching of antelopes for their wool continues. George Schaller calculated that in the 1990s, between 200,000 and 300,000 antelopes were killed.

George Schaller was behind the creation of the vast Changtang National Park and adjoining nature reserves in Qinghai (Hoh Xil) and Xinjiang, set up to protect the Tibetan Antelope. However, these are largely 'paper parks'—they look good on paper, but in fact are being exploited by mining and damming corporations. Poaching of Tibetan antelopes continues, though on a much smaller scale, with miners seeking extra income from shooting Tibetan Antelopes for their underwool and horns.

Are you a good detective?

Can you name the ten Tibetan animals here from their footprints?

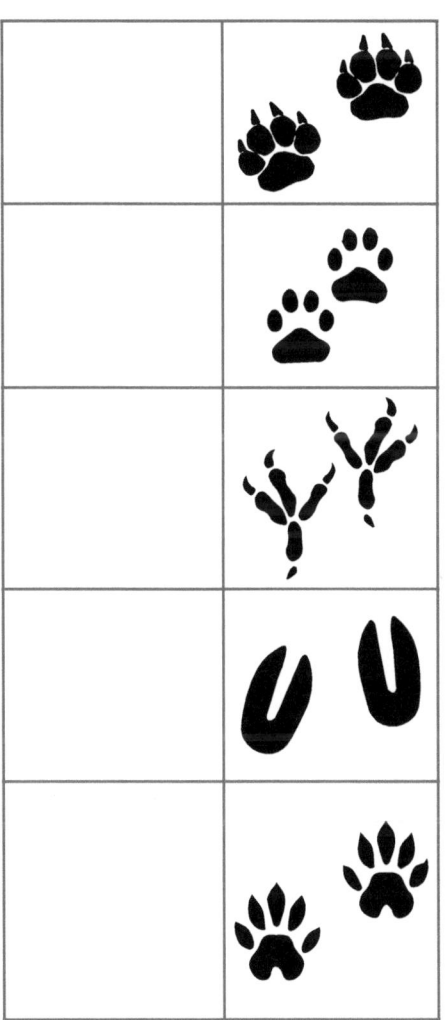
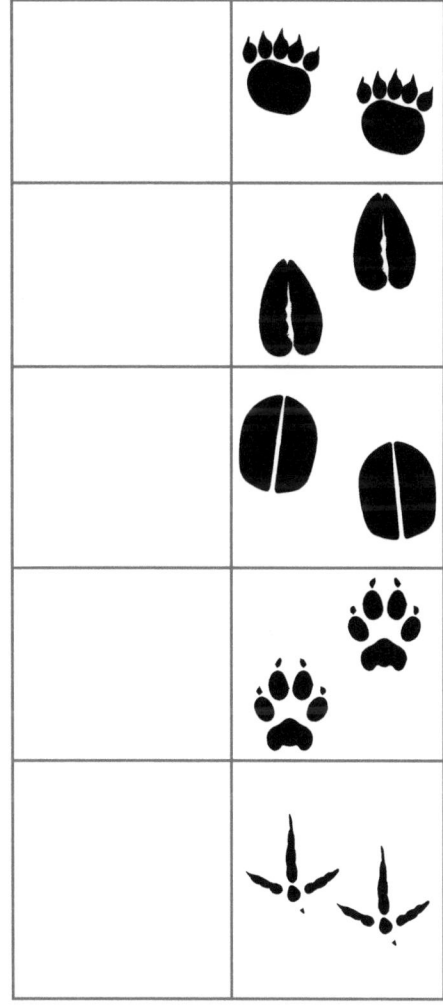

Let's talk about... IMPACT

Exploring environment issues related to the Tibetan Plateau—

including Tibet, Sikkim, Ladakh, Nepal and Bhutan—by animal:

Snow Leopard
Impact of gold mining. Poaching for pelts and Traditional Chinese Medicine. Snow Leopards killing livestock because their range is reduced. Insurance for herders against Snow Leopard attacks on their livestock.

Himalayan Griffon
Not all animals are pretty, or cute, or cuddly. But the ugly ones may have important roles to play. What is the Griffon's role and how important is this role? Secondary poisoning of Griffons from eating animals fed with Diclofenac.

Tibetan Antelope
Human greed for *shahtoosh*, Tibetan Antelope underwool: how can antelope poaching be stopped? How to shut down this illegal trade? Tibetan Antelope horns, after being ground up, are used for traditional medicine cures, but no proof this actually works.

Red Panda
Deforestation: impact on animals that live in trees, including the Red Panda and bird species. Why does the Giant Panda command so much respect in China while other bear species do not? The Red Panda is poached in India and smuggled into China, where it ends up in the pet trade and at private resorts. Yet this is an endangered animal.

Tibetan Brown Bear
Traditional Chinese Medicine (TCM) exploitation of animals. Does TCM using animal parts actually work? Is it effective when using bear bile? Why not just use synthetic medicines? China has great respect for the famous Giant Panda Bear, which is well-protected and treated well. Why are other bears like the Moon Bear and Brown Bear treated so horribly and held in cages?

Takin
The Himalayan Tahr's dilemma—overheating with big hairy coat on. Can animals adapt fast enough to climate change? How many generations does it take to adapt? Rescuing other species: will some species attempt to rescue other species from harm? What's in it for them? Can one animal species be friends with another animal species?

Wild Yak

Trouble on the grasslands of Tibet—introduction of Chinese fencing, removal of nomads and resettlement, removal of yaks to slaughterhouses. Yak grazing and grasslands relationship—the two have interacted for millennia. Contaminated river water—due to mining such as Lithium extraction, Amdo. Story mentions yaks going to market, which means they will be sold for meat and sent to slaughterhouses. Tibetan nomads depend on live yaks to get milk, butter, cheese and yak-hair. A dead yak is of no use to a nomad. There is a an anti-slaughterhouse movement in Tibet.

Tibetan Sand Fox

Black soot from burning of coal—impact on melting glaciers. Coal burning causes global warming. Creeping desertification and grasslands degradation in Tibet, due to Chinese mining. Coal mining at Muli, Amdo, inside a national nature reserve. China's long-term Pika poisoning campaign on the grassland of Tibet—is it necessary? Does it work? Surely predators can keep Pikas numbers in check? Impact of secondary poisoning on predators. Are China's national parks genuine—or are they Paper Parks, on paper only?

Smooth-coated Otter

China's megadam building on the rivers of Tibet and beyond in Nepal and other nations: Chinese built and financed. Impact of dams on fish migration and sediment for plants.

Black-necked Crane

How can youth be best educated to respect animals and their place on this planet? Over 50 percent of Bhutan's land area has been set aside for national parks, nature reserves and wildlife corridors. Can this success inspire other nations to preserve biodiversity? Why does biodiversity matter?

Can you spot the Himalayan Red Fox in this photo?
Why does the Red Fox look confused? The photo is from Muli, NE Tibet: it shows grasslands, coal-mining trucks, and snowcapped peaks.

Drawn by Samdol Lhamo, TCV

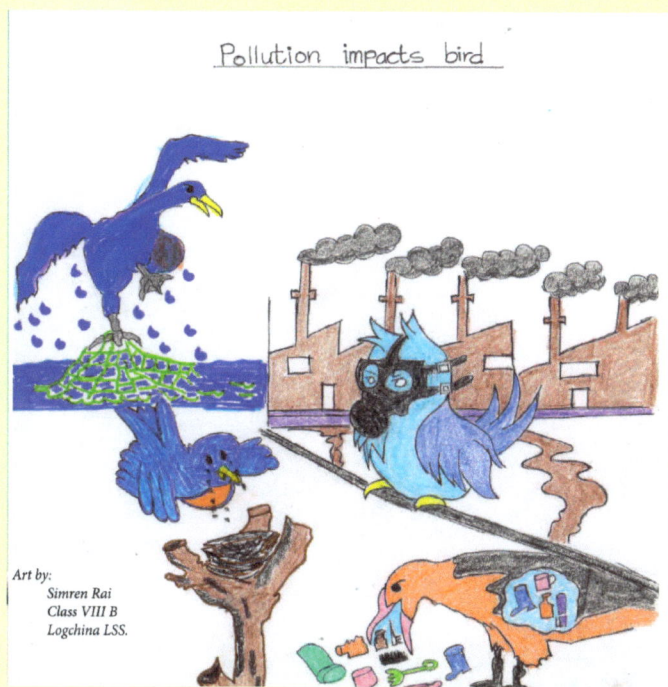

Message from the birds of Bhutan: an eighth-grader from Bhutan takes a sobering look at the problems that birds face due to human impact. Bhutan has over 670 species of birds. Bhutan has banned the use of plastic bags, so one less source of pollution.

Given a list of animals, with instructions to pick one and draw that animal as part of a competition, TCV student Jigme Gurung decided to paint all of them! Can you identify the animals drawn above?

An EXTRAordinary TAIL

No, this is not an optical illusion. The Snow Leopard has an enormous bushy tail, used to stabilize acrobatic leaps. At night, the tail is wrapped around the body and face to withstand freezing temperatures.
What other uses can that bushy tail be put to?
Find out on the following page—with imaginative uses!

Uses of the Snow Leopard's Really Long Tail

As a blanket

For balance

Snowboarding

Multiple bookmarks

Babysitting

Just some warm company over coffee

Paunch concealer

Animals may not talk much, but they have other ways of communicating...

Can you think of examples? What about the use of scent to get a message across? Scan the QR code below to listen to six Tibetan animal vocalizations. vimeo.com/590810113

TIBETAN ANIMAL Activity Book

with 14 pages of puzzles, games and quizzes about Tibetan animals: download the PDF free from:
naomicrose.com/books/snow-leopard-prowls/

Where Snow Leopard Prowls

Hardcover book about the wild animals of Tibet by Naomi C. Rose, written and illustrated by the author. Great introduction for young readers, aged 7 to 10. The author's website carries details of other Tibetan titles, and free activity material for ages 4 and up.

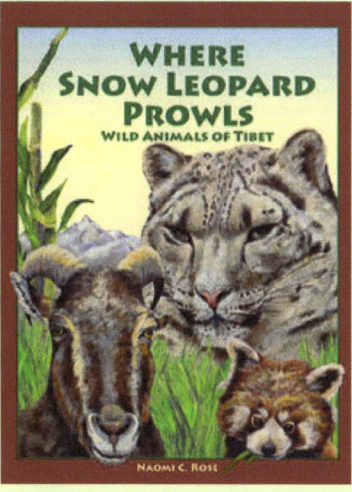

Books, Inspiration

A Wild Child's Guide to Endangered Animals
Author and illustrator Millie Marotta says she is hoping the book will tempt young readers to take a lifelong interest in wildlife conservation and show them there are things everyone can do to help, right now.

Our Animal Neighbours
Tibetan Buddhist monk Matthieu Ricard and writer Jason Gruhl make the case for compassion and empathy for all living creatures—the furry, slimy and the prickly—in this kids' book, illustrated by Becca Hall.

When the Buddha was an Elephant
There are a handful of versions of the ancient *Jataka Tales* published in English. This book features 36 animal wisdom stories on the former lives of the Buddha, retold by Mark McGinnis, with full-colour illustration. Suits ages 5 to 8+.

Where the River Runs Gold
Sita Brahmachari has created an adventure story set in a terrifying caste-divided, dystopian world in which bees have long disappeared and children must labour on farms to pollinate crops.

How to Save the Whole Stinkin' Planet
This laugh-out-loud book by the TV presenter, science communicator, and Captain Planet devotee Lee Constable covers topics from compost to button mending, and it's packed with quizzes and science experiments you can do at home. This book succeeds masterfully in demonstrating to kids the many ways they can reduce their carbon footprint, while also having a good giggle.

GET INVOLVED!
Young Climate Activists making a  difference

Licypriya Kangujam
Licypriya is the 2019 winner of World Children Peace Prize Award, the Nobel Prize for youth. She was 8 years old at the time. She won the Indian Peace Prize the same year, and addressed delegates at the UN Climate Conference in 2019 in Madrid—the youngest ever to do so. As an environmental activist, she takes time from school to protest outside the Indian Parliament, calling on the government to pass a climate law.

Greta Thunberg
In November 2018, Swedish teen Greta Thunberg initiated the school strike for climate movement, which saw over 50,000 people from 100 countries rally together in a call for action. Four months later, 1.4 million students from around the world participated in school strikes. Greta's speeches, including her fierce calls to action at both the UN and UK parliament, have been collected in a single book titled *No One Is Too Small to Make a Difference*. It's a small but mighty manifesto on the destruction wrought by prior generations, and the drastic and immediate action required to protect future generations.
fridaysforfuture.org
Fridays for Future is about involving kids to take action for climate change. This is Greta Thunberg's initiative to get a global movement rolling.

Youth to Power: Your Voice and How to Use it
This book is a step-by-step guide for becoming a youth activist for any cause. Written by Jamie Margolin, who co-founded Zero Hour, a youth-led nonprofit that advocates for climate action and environmental justice in the US. Check the website: *thisiszerohour.org*

If every 8-year-old in the world is taught meditation, we will eliminate violence from the world within one generation.
— HH Dalai Lama

Photo: Tenzin Choejor / OHHDL

INSPIRATION
from HH Dalai Lama

seelearning.emory.edu
Emory University's **SEE Learning Curriculum** is based on the vision of His Holiness the 14th Dalai Lama to see a world where every individual, irrespective of religion, can learn about Ethics and Emotional development.

Happiness
A comic book based on HH Dalai Lama's book *Ethics for the New Millennium*. Author Dr Barnali Verma exposes children to the compassionate teachings of His Holiness in a child-friendly pictorial manner.

The Seed of Compassion
Published in 2020, this is the first book written by HH Dalai Lama that directly talks to a young audience. He shares lessons of peace and compassion, told through stories of his own childhood. Lavishly illustrated by artist Bao Luu.

Cross-language
connections

SPECIAL THANKS to Geshe Lhakdor, Director of the LTWA in Dharamsala, for the motivation to see this book through to its final stages with his request for additional stories. And to Dadon, for translating this work into the Tibetan language. This book was created in English. Reading both Tibetan and English versions can help with language acquisition.

Tibetan, Dzongkha & Sanskrit names used in this book—and their meanings...

Snow Leopard	**Kaba** = a Tibetan word for 'snow' **Dorjee** = sceptre that is symbolic of spiritual strength and compassion
Red Panda	**Tashi** = auspicious, prosperity **Lolha** = good mind goddess (contraction of Lobsang + Lhamo) **Bhuti** = one who brings children **Jorten** = one who is wealthy
Himalayan Griffon	**Karlha** = star goddess (contraction of Karma + Lhamo) **Vikram** = victory/ bravery in Sanskrit
Tibetan Antelope	**Loden** = intelligent, smart **Gangze** = beautiful snowy **Khandro** = celestial dancer
Tibetan Brown Bear	**Barno** = sharp claws **Wangmo** = powerful woman **Xi-Xi** = 'happy-happy' in Chinese, named after the president **Jigme** = fearless one **Wangdu** = brings under control, conqueror
Takin	**Kinley** = good at everything (Dzongkha) **Marmuk** = 'reddish-brown' in Dzongkha **Tara** = goddess of compassion (Sanskrit)
Wild Yak	**Rogtur** = yak with shiny black hair **Dhongkar** = big white patch on forehead **Kargyan** = ornament of the stars **Yanglha** = goddess dispensing happiness
Tibetan Sand Fox	**Zinon** = strong sense of smell **Chimi** = close to Tibetan for 'cat' (*shimi*). Chime means 'immortal': this wild cat was thought to be extinct in Nepal and Bhutan but has shown up on camera-traps again. **Lhakpa** = fleet-footed **Yeshey** = gifted with heavenly knowledge, wise
Smooth-coated Otter	**Lumo** = female water-spirit or *klu* **Nanda** = short for Ananda, chief of the nagas in Sanskrit
Black-necked Crane	**Karma** = Sanskrit for cause and effect of action, fate. Also Tibetan for 'star' **Pema** = Tibetan for 'lotus flower.'

About the illustrator

Tenzin Choekyi was born in India. She grew up in Shillong and moved to Dharamsala. While recovering from an illness as a teen, she found drawing animals to be her great escape. This turned into a passion for art and drawing that she has pursued ever since. Her formal art training has been completion of a five-year course in Thangka painting.

About the cartoonist

Rohan Chakravarty is an award-winning cartoonist and illustrator from India. He is creator of *Green Humour*, a series of cartoons, comics and illustrations on wildlife and nature conservation—which appear in newspapers, magazines and journals, particularly in India. His cartoons and illustrations have been used for projects and campaigns on wildlife awareness and conservation. His best-known book is *Green Humour for a Greying Planet* (India Penguin, 2021). The animals that Rohan depicts include Tibetan species that live in India's northern Himalayan regions.

About the author

Michael Buckley is a Canadian writer and filmmaker with a strong interest in Tibet and Tibetan regions. He has travelled widely in the Tibetan world—to Tibet, Mongolia, Bhutan, Sikkim and Ladakh. He is editor of *This Fragile Planet: His Holiness the Dalai Lama on Environment*. And author of *Meltdown in Tibet*, a book about China's destruction of ecosystems on the Tibetan Plateau. *Tibet, Disrupted* is a photo companion to this—a digital photobook available online. He is filmmaker for three short documentaries about environment issues in Tibet. He has written a dozen books about the Himalayan and Southeast Asian regions, including *Tibet: the Bradt Travel Guide*.
More information at these websites:
MeltdowninTibet.com
WildYakFilms.com
Himmies.com

Author Michael Buckley with school-kids rehearsing the Crane Dance at Gangtey Gompa in Bhutan

Author's Story

In late 2014, I was invited to a meeting of the Elephant Society in Hong Kong. This is a conservation group, supported by well-heeled patrons, with a lot of work to do. Because Hong Kong is the epicentre of the trade in ivory—a trade that is sending elephants hurtling toward extinction. Life-size elephant photos graced the walls of the venue. The speaker that night was seasoned wildlife activist Jane Goodall, in her eighties.

And at the other end of the age spectrum, standing next to her, barely peeping over the podium, was an eight-year-old elephant activist. Eight years old! Jane Goodall explained that nobody pushed this girl into activism. She simply saw a program on TV about poaching of elephants for their tusks and turned to her parents and said: *That's not right! That is so wrong!* The young girl gave a passionate short speech about how she wants to grow up in a world where she could see wild elephants. With tusks on them. Such magnificent creatures. There was not a dry eye in the house. Donations rained down.

And I was so inspired, I decided that night that I would write a children's book. About endangered Tibetan animals. Because I think youth like that kid hold the key to saving the planet. They are fearless.

Heartfelt Thanks

My gratitude to John Negru at Sumeru Books for his patience in seeing this book into print. Publishing these days walks a fine line for sustainability, and John Negru is willing to take chances. Thanks to eagle-eyed Riina Tamm, who read the early versions of this book, and the later versions—in fact, all the versions. Visual input for this book comes from a handful of creative artists: my thanks to Tenzin Choekyi for her beautfiul illustrations, Rohan Chakravarty for his imaginative cartoons, Roger Handling for the great cover, and Isabel Arnaud for wonderful book design ideas. And special thanks to the photographers with long lenses who contributed snapshots of these rare creatures—very difficult to get. This book went out to readers who offered invaluable feedback. None more so than the eight-year-old nephew of Tsechu Dolma, who demanded certain changes in the narrative. And by heck, those changes were made.

Copyright & Credits

The Snow Leopard's New Friend
by Michael Buckley
First Sumeru Books edition 2021
Copyright © 2021 Michael Buckley
All rights reserved
Protected by this Tibetan Mastiff

Book design: Isabel Arnaud
Proofreader: Riina Tamm
Readers: Patsie Lamarre, Tsechu Dolma, Bill Weir
Cover design: Roger Handling
Illustrator: Tenzin Choekyi
Cartoonist: Rohan Chakravarty / Green Humour
Photographers: Michael Buckley, Tenzin Choejor/OHHDL, Tshering Tobgay, Matteo Pistono, Joan Chadwick, Daniel Miller, Brian Harris
Other editions: *A modified digital version of this book is available at online platforms like Amazon, published by ThunderHorse Media. A Tibetan translation of this work has been published by the LTWA, Dharamsala, India, in both print and digital versions.*

The Sumeru Press Inc.
sumeru-books.com

གསར་ཡོལ་གྲོགས་པོ་གསར་པ།

Library and Archives Canada Cataloguing in Publication

Title: The snow leopard's new friend / by Michael Buckley.
Names: Buckley, Michael, 1950- author.
Description: Includes bibliographical references.
Identifiers: Canadiana 20210282037 | ISBN 9781896559773 (softcover)
Subjects: LCSH: Animals—Tibet Region—Juvenile literature. | LCSH: Wildlife conservation—Tibet
  Region—Juvenile literature.
Classification: LCC QL307 .B83 2021 | DDC j591.951/5—dc23

www.ingramcontent.com/pod-product-compliance
Lightning Source LLC
Chambersburg PA
CBHW041547220426
43665CB00003B/58